VINALOGY

Wine basics with a twist!

Helena Nicklin

Published by New Generation Publishing in 2013

Copyright © Helena Nicklin 2013

First Edition

The author asserts the moral right under the Copyright, Designs and Patents Act 1988 to be identified as the author of this work.

All Rights reserved. No part of this publication may be reproduced, stored in a retrieval system or transmitted, in any form or by any means without the prior consent of the author, nor be otherwise circulated in any form of binding or cover other than that which it is published and without a similar condition being imposed on the subsequent purchaser.

www.newgeneration-publishing.com

To Hamish,

For all your creative help, love and support ... and also for being an awesome drinking partner.

Vin·al·o·gy
[*vin*-**nal**-*uh*-jee] *–noun, **plural*** -gies.

A vinous analogy that paints memorable pictures of anything wine-related.

Contents

Introduction   9

Chapter 1   HOW TO TACKLE THE SUBJECT OF WINE   11
Why wine is like a naked person

Chapter 2   THE VINALOGY   15
The top red and white grape varieties

Chapter 3   START SPEAKING WINE LANGUAGE   96
"Dead leaves and cow poo. In a good way."

Chapter 4   UNDERSTANDING A WINE LIST   98
* What you need to know
* Key terms you'll find on a label

Chapter 5   WINE FAQ   109
Answers to common wine questions

Chapter 6   TASTING WINE   119
* What to look for when you taste
* Tasting ideas to help you learn

Chapter 7   WINE TOP TRUMPS   125
Checklist of wines named after places and styles, not grapes

Introduction

Why is Cabernet the rugby player of the wine world?
How is Viognier like a tropical sun goddess?
Which grape is the ladyboy of Piedmont?

Winebird's VINALOGY is a beginner's wine guide with a difference.

Step one of the journey to wine knowledge nirvana should not be complicated winemaking details, but getting to know the key grape varieties: the building blocks of wine. The top ten red and white grapes are therefore the focus for this book and my 'Vinalogies' will help you familiarise yourself with them in a quirky, memorable way. Should you then want to know more, VINALOGY will point you in the right direction without ramming unnecessary facts and figures down your throat.

VINALOGY won't bang on about rootstocks, oak barrels or the name of the producer's dog, because all of that stuff can and should come later. Instead, it'll show you how to tackle the subject of wine as a total beginner, explain how to speak wine language like a pro, give you ideas for tastings to try at home and answer those frequently asked questions.

I wrote this book after leading countless tastings for people who entertain a lot, both professionally and socially. They wanted to know more about wine without getting bogged down in detail; to drink the stuff, not sit an exam in it! Together, we narrowed down what it was that the average wine drinker really wanted to know. Here it is on paper: the *real* wine basics. Information you can actually use.

PAH to dry facts!

winebird

The Caveat

For every rule, there is someone somewhere that breaks it and nowhere is this more true than in the hugely complex world of wine. What follows is therefore <u>deliberately generalised</u> to prevent information overload, so please bear this in mind!

Chapter 1

HOW TO TACKLE THE SUBJECT OF WINE
(Why wine is like a naked person)

Sometimes, we don't want all the information. Lees ageing? Malolactic fermentation? PAH! There are just four key elements to be aware of when you start to learn about wine. Concentrate on these, in this order, and you'll find that the finer details such as the effects of vintage and producer will crop up as and when they're relevant.

Here are those four key elements with a Vinalogy to help you remember them:

THE VINALOGY

Think of a bottle of wine as a person. Now think of them naked. Go on! No clothes but also, no make-up and natural, unruly hair, just as nature intended. What we have here is the raw material that forms the backbone of a person's appearance: the **DNA**. Sure, there are many things that can be done to tweak the way this person appears to the outside world: **clothes**, **haircut** and **make-up** being three key elements, but you'll never get too far away from what Mother Nature has produced...

1: THE NAKED BODY (Grape Variety)

The grape variety (or varieties) is your person, naked. Think **DNA**: the most important ingredient by far. This is because each *grape variety*, be it Malbec, Pinot Grigio or whatever, has its own individual, inherent characteristics, so will instantly give you the biggest hint about flavour, style and texture. Getting to know the major grape varieties is therefore absolutely where you should start when you want to learn about wine.

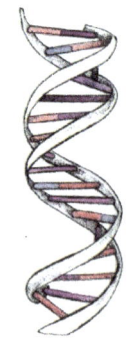

2: CLOTHES (Climate)

Next up, think **clothes**. In Winebird terms, this means *climate*. Just like clothes on a person, climate is the next most important element that can affect style. *Very* generally speaking, a grape grown in a cool climate (such as Northern Europe) will produce wines that are more restrained, lighter bodied, less alcoholic and less fruity than the exact same grape variety grown somewhere hot. See what I mean by comparing two wines made with the same grape from different places. You can find ideas about what to taste in **Chapter 6**.

3: HAIRCUT (Vineyard)

The next element to tweak the appearance of our wine body is **haircut.** Think pruning. Think *vineyard*! There are many things that can be done while the grapes are still growing to fine-tune the final wine style: cutting back leaves to increase sun exposure and aid ripening is one example (this means bigger, fruitier wines). Removing excess bunches to increase concentration in the remaining ones is another. Older vines are said to give wine more complexity and the type of **soil** is also said to have an effect on the texture and, occasionally, flavour of a wine. Roll some Chablis around your mouth, for example. Doesn't it feel a bit chalky? Guess why...

4: MAKE-UP (Winery)

After haircut, think **make-up.** In wine terms, this means *winemaking*: i.e. what happens in the winery after grapes have been harvested. Like a make-up artist working on a model, there are hundreds of things a winemaker can do to enhance a wine's best features and smooth out the flaws. They could add a touch of powder to increase acidity, for example, or a kiss of oak for spice and texture. The winemaker may even blend two or more grape varieties together to make an entirely different wine. (See **Chapter 5** for more on blends). The grape(s) should always still be recognisable underneath the slap, however.

So there you have it: the four main elements that affect the style of a wine. Now you know how to do it, let's start with element one: grape variety!

13

Chapter 2

THE VINALOGY
Top red and white grape varieties

Imagery and storytelling provide a much more effective way to remember things than memorising dry facts, and analogy lends itself beautifully to wine. There are literally thousands of grape varieties in the world, but relatively few that have truly international fame and appeal. I have chosen to introduce the ten white and ten red grapes that you are currently most likely to see in shops and restaurants. These are the ones to start with.

The *Tasting Tours* at the end of each Vinalogy are designed to guide you towards the most famous areas for producing the grape varieties mentioned, as well as a few areas that are not so famous but make styles you might want to try.

White Grapes

* Sauvignon Blanc
* Chardonnay
* Riesling
* Viognier
* Pinot Grigio aka Pinot Gris
* Semillon
* Gewürztraminer
* Albariño
* Chenin Blanc
* Melon de Bourgogne (Muscadet)

Red Grapes

* Cabernet Sauvignon
* Pinot Noir
* Merlot
* Syrah aka Shiraz
* Malbec
* Pinotage
* Tempranillo
* Sangiovese
* Zinfandel
* Nebbiolo

White Grape Vinalogies

SAUVIGNON BLANC

VINALOGY: The English Country Garden

Don't you just love crisp spring mornings? With the inevitable April showers, it's as if someone has spritzed the air with Sauvignon Blanc: the wine that tastes like an English country garden...

Breathe in the scent of **freshly cut grass**, **damp ferns** and **asparagus** in the vegetable patch. **Elderflower** and **gooseberry** bushes gracefully frame a **wet stone** path and the faint hint of classical music is just audible in the background. Ah, the peace and tranquillity! But what's this?

The rain has stopped, the temperature is rising and someone has turned the volume on the stereo right up to the max. What's more, they've added some bongo drums to the mix. The garden has taken on the feel of a **tropical** fiesta, and I swear the plants have grown bigger. Look what happens when you add some sun!

***

Sauvignon Blanc: arguably the most recognisable white grape variety around. It is the Marmite of wines; you either love it or you hate it. Along with its zesty, grass and wet stone flavours come distinctive aromas that its fans describe as elderflower, its dissenters as cat pee!

Sauvignon is the pale yellow, green-tinged white that's always first to be picked out in a line-up. You may prefer it in its reserved, English garden mode, in which case you'd head straight for a cooler climate such as northern France. But if you're more of a party fiend, digging the louder, more tropical, vibe, then head somewhere with a little more sunshine, like New Zealand or Chile.

FACT: Sauvignon Blanc is the only grape variety used to make the famous French white wines of *Sancerre* and *Pouilly Fumé*.

TIP: Un-oaked Sauvignon Blanc is best drunk young (within a couple of years of the vintage), so don't keep it too long.

18

SAUVIGNON BLANC TASTING TOUR

Sauvignon Blanc 1: *France's Loire Valley* is Sauvignon's true home, and the villages of *Sancerre* and *Pouilly Fumé* are two of the most famous names. This is where you'll find classic, country garden aromas in a reserved, refined style with a particular, mineral tang. Wines from Pouilly Fumé also often have a flinty smokiness to them thanks to the soil ('fumé' means 'smoked' in French).

Sauvignon Blanc 2: Sauvignon has a permanent holiday home in *Marlborough, New Zealand.* Equally happy here as it is in France, the flavour volume is turned right up and someone has brought out the tinned asparagus and tropical fruit! You can't do Sauvignon Blanc without trying one from Marlborough.

Sauvignon Blanc 3: For amazing value, with more savoury, smoked grapefruit notes (and sometimes, a little bit of farmer's armpit), head to cool-climate *Chile. Casablanca Valley* and *Leyda Valley* are two regions to look out for.

Sauvignon Blanc is...
- Pale lemon-green in colour
- Very rarely oaked
- All about cut grass, wet stone, elderflower (or cat pee!) and, sometimes, tropical fruit
- Star grape of Sancerre & France & Marlborough, New Zealand

CHARDONNAY

VINALOGY: The 'Kate' of the wine world

Think back to your school days. Weren't there always at least four people in your class with the same first name? In my year, it was *Kate*: fat ones; skinny ones; drippy ones; foreign ones, you name it! Variations on a theme of *Kate* were popular the world over.

It was hard to work out how to feel about *Kates,* because just as you had decided that you hated the name because of spotty-faced Kate who smelt of potato, you met supermodel-in-training Kate who had a perm and older friends who could get into nightclubs. Suddenly, you wanted to name all your future children Kate. Even the boys.

***

Well, Chardonnay is the wine version of *Kate*. The sheer number of styles you'll find worldwide can make it difficult to pin down your thoughts on the matter. After all, nearly every wine-producing region in the world has a go at growing it! And as styles of this wine go, Chardonnay moves from the sublime to the ridiculous, being responsible for some of the greatest white wines in the world. Climate and winemaking techniques may leave their mark, but the key elements will always be there somewhere: look for a **golden** colour, **ripe melon** flavour and a **fuller body** than many other white varieties such as Sauvignon Blanc. **Vanilla** and **buttery** notes are also good indicators that the wine is a Chardonnay. Try it un-oaked for a true reading of its merits.

FACT: 'Blanc de Blancs' Champagne means it's made from 100% Chardonnay and the style is usually more ethereal, fine boned and delicate than the wines traditionally blended with the red Champagne grapes (Pinot Noir and Pinot Meunier).

Chardonnay is...
- Yellow-gold in colour
- Often associated with oak, but equally delicious without it
- All about melon, butter and vanilla flavours
- Star white grape of Burgundy, France but famous worldwide

CHARDONNAY TASTING TOUR

Chardonnay 1: *Kate, the model.* Lean, cool and understated. This style is elegant and super dry. Celebrated the world over, there's only one *Chablis* and it comes from the *French* region of the same name. Don't be that person who 'loves Chablis but hates Chardonnay!'

 **Chardonnay 2**: *Katie, the centrefold.* Big, buxom and bursting with fruit! The *Californian* style of Chardonnay generally has a rich and creamy, vanilla pudding feel. Cheaper versions are often 'enhanced' with oak chips, but the top-end wines tend to use oak barrels, giving unctuous caramel flavours.

Chardonnay 3: *Cat, the girl next door.* A safe, easy-drinking crowd-pleaser with just enough melony character and curves to keep everyone happy. Get your lips around a mid-priced offering from *Chile*, *New Zealand*, *South Africa*, *Australia*.

Chardonnay 4: *Katherine, the Oscar winner.* With plenty of complexity, character and sophistication, throw a little money at a top-end white from the *Burgundy* region of *France* ('Bourgogne' in French). Try a Puligny-Montrachet or a Pouilly-Fuissé for starters. 'White Burgundy' will be 100% Chardonnay, 99% of the time.

RIESLING

VINALOGY: Runways & Rubber Boots!

A German supermodel in **lime**-green **rubber** wellies. What a picture! This kooky vision of loveliness sums up what Riesling is all about. With long, **lean** limbs and golden curls like **spun sugar**, this fresh-faced beauty can take barrelfuls of sugar without ever becoming flabby. Suiting any style you throw at her, from **über dry** to **sweet** and pretty, she'll always exude that inimitable character that could never be anyone else. A national heroine for her **distinctive**, **world-famous** beauty, Riesling is the German supermodel of the wine world!

Think freshly squeezed lime with the faint aroma of hot rubber. In a good way. These are the classic markers for the distinctive Riesling grape variety and they get increasingly bold with age. Try it lip-pursingly dry or with a sprinkling of sugar, but even as a full-on dessert-style wine, Riesling's high acidity – just like a supermodel's metabolism – will give it that clean and lean feel despite the sweetness.

One problem that wine drinkers often have with Riesling is understanding the label on the classic German wines; there's a lot of information and it can be tricky to know how dry or sweet the wine is going to be. Some winemakers now use 'dry', 'medium dry', 'medium-sweet' and 'sweet' on their labels, which helps, but otherwise, there's a fair bit of translation involved. I've written more about this on my blog. For more information, search for 'German labels' on Winebird.org.

FACT: German wines also have a quality classification based on the ripeness of the grapes at harvest. While this is not a general indication of the final sweetness, it will give you a hint towards the wine's body. Again, see my blog for more details.

> Riesling is...
> - All styles from bone dry up to super sweet
> - Always fresh because of its super-high acidity
> - All about lime rubber and, sometimes, petrol flavours!
> - Star grape of Germany and a star of Alsace, France

RIESLING TASTING TOUR

Riesling 1: *Germany* is Riesling's spiritual home, so start here! If you're after a wine that's delicate in body, with just a touch of lime, flowery aromas and a hint of sweetness, try a *Kabinett*-style Riesling with one or two years of age on it. For more body try the *Spätlese* or *Auslese* styles.

 **Riesling 2:** For something dry, but fuller in body and with riper and rounder fruit, head to *Alsace* in *France* to experience their very different, but also classic style of Riesling.

Riesling 3: If you want a wine that's viscous and bone-dry with lashings of quirky lime and rubber flavours, head to *Clare Valley* or *Eden Valley* in *Australia*. This is your supermodel looking good in a tight PVC catsuit!

Riesling 4: For something totally different once again, head for that crazy name and grab a *Trockenbeerenauslese* or an *Eiswein*. You'll be blown away by the explosive, unctuous, tropical flavours that, despite the sugar, manage not to be cloying thanks to the grape's refreshingly high acidity. A delicious pudding wine.

VIOGNIER

VINALOGY: The Sun Goddess

Viognier is the grape that offers us a piece of tropical paradise in a bottle.

A bronzed, **golden** haired sun goddess stands with an **apricot** cocktail in hand. Skin glistening with **coconut oil**, she places a garland of **white flowers** around your neck. You inhale the delicate, **musky** scent as you take the glass. A burst of **fresh apricot** and **peach** explodes on your palate. The effect is seductive and delicious.

Introducing Viognier: a peachy little number that's enough to lift our spirits on the coldest of days with its full-bodied fruitiness and satisfying oily texture. The delightful weightiness also reminds us of white chocolate-covered apricots and musky pine kernels, all served on a bed of acacia blossom. Wow! Even a sun goddess can suffer from sunstroke though. With too much heat, Viognier can become 'flabby', i.e. lacking acidity and freshness. In the right conditions, however, she's tropical, floral and delicious!

FACT: There's a rather quirky style of *red* wine that involves adding a dash of Viognier to Syrah for intrigue and a splash of floral beauty. This is known as a 'Côte-Rôtie' style of wine because the practice started in the *Côte-Rôtie* appellation within France's Northern Rhône Valley.

Viognier is...
- Peachy gold in colour
- Full bodied and low in acidity with an oily texture
- All about apricot, acacia blossom and ripe peaches
- Star grape of Condrieu, in the Northern Rhône Valley, France

VIOGNIER TASTING TOUR

Viognier 1: Save up your pennies and find a *Condrieu* from the production zone of the same name in France's Northern *Rhône Valley*, Viognier's spiritual home. Condrieu is 100% Viognier and has layers of complexity combined with elegance and power. Think honeysuckle, banana cream and spiced apricots. It's got the whole package.

Viognier 2: Next up, head to *Southern Australia*. Oz is Viognier's adopted home and the *Eden Valley* is where it all started. Here, the wines are perky and peachy, packed full of floral and fruity flavours.

Viognier 3+: For relatively inexpensive and easy-drinking Viognier, banish those winter blues and head to the *Languedoc-Roussillon* region of *France*. *Chile's* cooler regions such as the *Casablanca Valley* are also offering some gorgeously powerful and aromatic versions of Viognier. Look out for a spicy kick on the finish!

31

PINOT GRIGIO (aka PINOT GRIS)

VINALOGY: The Flat-Pack Furniture Grape

When we're old enough to start purchasing furniture, flat-pack is usually the way to go. **Inexpensive** and **functional**, it feels so exciting and grown up at the time! All those **neutral, clean lines** and just the occasional flash of character on those beige curtains. It doesn't require much thought. There's a **recognisable brand** out there for you that does the job with minimum fuss until you're ready to graduate onto something with a little more personality and, perhaps, a higher price tag.

There is a certain charm in not having to think about what you're drinking all the time and Pinot Grigio is so widely drunk now thanks to its neutral and inoffensive nature, that it feels like a brand in its own right! If you go beyond the average pub or restaurant wine list, however, you will find some that are a little more 'hand made' and characterful, though you will see this reflected in the price. It can make a rather lovely wine with **yeasty**, **salted almond** and subtle **pear** characteristics. You just need to know where to look!

FACT: Pinot Grigio and Pinot Gris are the same grape variety; 'gris' just means 'grey' in French (the skin is greyish pink), whereas 'grigio' is the Italian word.

FACT: Just as Shiraz is the same grape as Syrah but makes wines of a different style, so Pinot Gris shows another side to Pinot Grigio. When a wine is labelled as Pinot Gris, the wine has a subtle pink hue, more floral aromatics and a sweeter ripeness than the stony, neutral character of the Pinot Grigio style.

Pinot Grigio is...
- Very pale lemon in colour
- Moderate in alcohol and body
- All about subtlety with almond and stony notes
- A star grape of the Veneto, Italy

Pinot Gris is...
- Pale lemon with a pink hue
- Aromatic and floral
- About citrus character and perceived sweetness
- A star in Alsace, France

PINOT GRIGIO / PINOT GRIS
TASTING TOUR

Pinot Grigio 1: For starters, head straight to Pinot Grigio's home in the *Veneto* region of *Northern Italy*. This is the flat-pack version: clean and neutral with some subtle, stone fruit character if you're lucky. Highly gluggable, if not terribly inspiring.

Pinot Grigio 2: Stay in *Italy*, but try the region of *Friuli* (full name: Colli Orientali del Friuli). Wines from here have a little more weight and character than those in the Veneto generally, but they will probably be more expensive.

Pinot Grigio 3: *California* produces some delicious, round and ripe Pinot Grigios with real character and texture. It's like a midway point between Grigio and Gris!

***

Pinot Gris 1: A classic area for the Pinot Gris style is *Alsace* in *France*, where wines are more weighty and creamy, showing off some lovely floral notes.

Pinot Gris 2: For inexpensive and very cheerful versions of the aromatic, flowery Pinot Gris style, try wines from the *Famatina Valley* in *Argentina*.

Pinot Gris 3: *America's North West* (*Oregon* in particular) is a fabulous place for the Pinot Gris style of wine with white flower aromas and spicy, baked pear flavours. It's another great midway point between the Gris and Grigio style. Prices tend to justifiably be quite high here.

35

SEMILLON

VINALOGY: The Tennis Player

Oh, the British players at Wimbledon: silent and **neutral** in their tennis whites, **angular** with youth and muscle, hair **waxed** neatly into place, soberly sipping the famous **lime** juice cordial on the sidelines. It's all rather, well, **clean**! The tennis is the focus, watched intently and in silence by those lucky enough to be there in SW19.

Come back to these players in a few years, however, and a transformation will have taken place. They may have retired but they're much more fun! We can now see a cracking personality and they've **filled out** a bit, **softening** slightly round the edges. In the commentary box, their dulcet tones are as comforting as **toast and honey**!

***

Angular, lime flavoured and, quite frankly, pretty neutral in its youth, Semillon comes out of its shell when the bottle is a few years old, developing real character. A weighty, waxy mouthfeel and an intriguing flavour profile of lime, honey and toast (often mistaken for oak, which Semillon rarely sees) is your reward for the wait. And, like a professional tennis player, Semillon makes a particularly good partner for mixed doubles, which is why you'll very often see it blended with Sauvignon Blanc. Sauvignon adds aromatics and a much-needed zip to Semillon's waxy, soft weight, so together they make the perfect team.

FACT: In France, there is an accent on the 'e': Sémillon. Elsewhere in the world, it loses it!

FACT: Heard of Sauternes? This sweet wine from France is arguably the most famous Sémillon-Sauvignon blend in the world.

> **Semillon is...**
> - Straw yellow and green in colour
> - Has a thickish, waxy consistency
> - All about neutrality in youth, then limey and toasty despite lack of oak
> - A star in Australia's Hunter Valley and in Bordeaux, France

SEMILLON TASTING TOUR

Semillon 1: *Australia's Hunter Valley* in *New South Wales* is the key destination for classy, very dry, 100% Semillon wines. Try a new vintage next to one that's at least four years old to see the difference that age makes to the wine's personality.

Semillon 2: The regions of *Bordeaux* and *Bergerac* in *South West France* make more subtle, dry Sémillon, which is usually, but not always, blended with Sauvignon Blanc. Notice the 'é' when it's French!

Semillon 3: *New Zealand* produces some very grassy, fresh versions of Semillon. Come here for the anti-fruit bomb.

Semillon 4: If it's a dessert style of wine you're after, then head to *South Africa* or *Washington State* for wines full of unctuous tropical fruit that are as fresh as several daisies. For a classic French Sémillon-Sauvignon blend, however, you can't ignore the famous wines of *Sauternes* within the production area of *Bordeaux*.

GEWÜRZTRAMINER

VINALOGY: The Exotic Market

Have you ever lost yourself in the heady aromas of an exotic food market? Delicate **pink roses** frame the path as you enter, their scent mingling with the **cinnamon**, **ginger** and **nutmeg** from the **spice** stall on the corner. From the fruit section, captivating aromas of fresh **lychee** and **orange peel** drift towards you as you squeeze a **soft** square of **Turkish delight** between your fingers. The air is so **perfumed**, you feel a little giddy as you drink it all in!

Welcome to Gewürztraminer (pronounced 'guh-vertstrammy-nah'); aka 'Gewürz' or just 'Traminer'. Subtly pink in colour thanks to its skin, you can always recognise this exotic, fragrant beauty a mile off, no matter where in the world it's grown. Lychee, rose petal, ginger and orange peel best describe its distinctive aroma, and its ripe, well-rounded body and low acidity make it feel like a soft-skinned beauty. Dab some behind your ears and you'll be set for the night!

Gewürztraminer is the grape that sounds "well hard" but it isn't at all: it's just quite hard to say, which partly explains why it's not nearly as popular as it should be. Give it a try!

FACT: 'Gewürz' is the German word for spice and Tramin is the Tyrolean village where the Traminer grape is said to hail from. Gewürztraminer is therefore a spicy version of Traminer.

FACT: When written in French, there is no umlaut accent on the 'U'. It's just 'Gewurztraminer'.

Gewürztraminer is...
- Subtly rose-pink in colour
- Full bodied and aromatic but with low acidity
- All about lychee, rose and ginger
- One of the star grapes of Alsace, France

GEWÜRZTRAMINER TASTING TOUR

Gew<u>u</u>rztraminer 1: Head straight to *Alsace* in *France* to sample a classic, powerful and dry style of Gewurztraminer. Note the lack of umlaut accent on the 'U'.

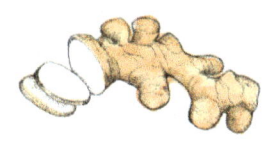

Gewürztraminer 2: Pitch your Alsatian against wines from *Gisborne*, *New Zealand* for similarly powerful styles that include some intriguing off-dry versions.

Gewürztraminer 3: They may be harder to find, but if you can, try some Gewürztraminer from *Oregon* in the *USA* for serious wines with a beautiful balance of all the grape's best characteristics.

Gewürztraminer 4: Gewürz. can be dry or off-dry, but if it's real sweetness you want, go for a *late harvest*, dessert-style wine from any of these places. Just make sure you check the label to know which one you're getting!

ALBARIÑO

VINALOGY: The Mermaid

Stormy seas and siren songs! Imagine the thunder rumbling in **Galicia** on Spain's North Western Coast as the waves crash onto the rocks. Flashes of sunlight stream through the clouds bathing everything in warmth and light, and for those brief moments you catch the scent of **ripening lemons** mingling with **wet rocks** and **sea spray**. Against this backdrop, you spot a figure in the distant waves: a mermaid, **voluptuous**, with **golden** hair and a **firm**, **peachy** complexion. She's **intense** and **hypnotic** as she sings her siren song.

Introducing Albariño: the mermaid; the 'wine of the sea!' With zingy, high acidity, she is the perfect match for seafood. Her intense aromatics of spicy peach and lemon are not too dissimilar to Viognier, but her mineral, ocean-like tang, her fine, light body and coastal freshness (thanks the cool of her Galician home) give her away. Her thick, firm skin also offers up a tell-tale bitterness on the finish.

FACT: Albariño is also very well known in Portugal, where it is called 'Alvarinho', helping to make it the flagship white grape of the Iberian Peninsula. Its popularity is increasing so rapidly, however, that we are now also starting to see small plantings of it elsewhere around the world.

Albariño is...
- The golden, seafood wine
- Crisp and fresh but with citrusy curves
- All about minerals, spicy peach and lemon with a bitter kick
- The star white grape of Galicia, Spain

ALBARIÑO TASTING TOUR

Albariño 1: For the white that's taking the world by storm, look no further than the *Rías Baixas* (pronounced Ree-yas By-shas) region in *Galicia* on the coast of *North-western Spain*.

Albariño 2: Known as 'Alvarinho' across the border in *Portugal*, this grape makes similar styled wines in *Monção*, a sub-region of *Minho* where they are part of the famous Vinho Verde wines.

Albariño 3+: While the Iberian Peninsula is the true home of this intensely refreshing style of wine, very interesting and impressive, often fuller-bodied, examples can also be found in pockets of *California*, *Oregon* and *Australia*.

47

CHENIN BLANC

VINALOGY: The Beekeeper

In the **dewy** sunshine of his private **orchard**, our beekeeper tends to the little **honeybees** in his **lanolin** suit. We're never quite sure who's underneath that veil: is he skinny and nondescript, or could he be softer and fuller figured? Is it even the same person every time? True fame has so far eluded the beekeeper, as we can never quite pin him down. And surely, he must be slightly **masochistic**; this is a job with a **sting** in the tail!

Chenin Blanc likes pain: he needs to be severely pruned to get results or he ends up insipid with a damp wool flavour and that famous, stingingly high acidity all too apparent. Get it right and add a bit of sunshine, however, and you'll be rewarded with honeydew melon notes, a touch of quince or pineapple and a pleasant, beeswax feel.

This grape of many faces makes still, sparkling and dessert wines that are dry, sweet or full-on syrupy in style, though it's only a very small amount of these gloriously honeyed *moelleux* dessert wines that have achieved any real fame. They can age for years thanks to Chenin's screechingly high acidity.

FACT: In its original Loire Valley home, Chenin is better known as 'Pineau de la Loire', whereas in its New World home-from-home in South Africa, it's also known as 'Steen'.

FACT: South America also has a lot of (fairly unexciting) Chenin Blancs, which are more often than not labelled as 'Pinot Blanco'.

Chenin Blanc is…
- Pale, sunshine yellow in colour
- Extremely versatile, making still, sparkling, sweet and dry wines
- All about beeswax, melon, honey and lanolin
- The star white grape of the Eastern Loire Valley and South Africa

CHENIN BLANC TASTING TOUR

Chenin Blanc 1: For classy, classic dry and still Chenin, look no further than *Savennières* in France's Eastern Loire Valley.

Chenin Blanc 2: If it's lusciously sweet Chenin you want, head to *Bonnezeaux*, *Quarts de Chaume* and the *Coteaux de Layon*, again in France's Loire Valley and look for a 'moelleux' style dessert wine.

Chenin Blanc 3: Sparkling Chenin can be found mainly in *Saumur* and *Vouvray*, again in the Loire Valley. Vouvray has a slightly fuller, richer style than Saumur.

Chenin Blanc 4: *South Africa* is generally the place to go for easy-drinking **table wines** as well as **sparkling** and **dessert** styles. The extra bit of heat here gives the wines softer, honeydew melon flavours.

MUSCADET

VINALOGY: Purity Personified in Porcelain

There's something different about Muscadet; it's almost otherworldly. The hairs on the back of your neck **prickle** in her presence. Like a porcelain angel in a long, **white chiffon** dress, Muscadet gives the impression of eternal **youth**. Maybe it's the **subtle** expression on that **delicate**, **fine-boned** face or the **crushed seashell** complexion? She is **purity** personified and there is only **one place** she could possibly hail from.

Muscadet wears no make-up; it is not a show-off wine. Made to be drunk young (and certainly within three years of production), Muscadet is a white wine that is only found in one place: France's Loire Valley. Almost water-white, it has a super-dry, crushed seashell freshness and chalky texture when at its best. The neutral, squeaky-clean style is as pure as the driven snow, offering just the subtlest suggestion of salinity that hints at its Atlantic coastal hometown. Muscadet made in the 'Sur-Lie' style (see Tasting Tour) often has a prickle of CO2 that adds to the freshness and effortlessly cleans the palate. If you love the pure dryness of Chablis, a decent Muscadet will be right up your street!

FACT: Muscadet is the French wine that's the exception to the rule, being named after a certain musky **style**, rather than a grape variety or region. The grape used is always 'Melon de Bourgogne', as it originally hailed from Burgundy (Bourgogne).

Muscadet is...
- Almost water-white in colour
- Often has a prickle of CO2
- All about chalky, neutral and saline flavours
- The star wine of the Nantais in France's Loire Valley

MUSCADET TASTING TOUR

France, France and well, France! In fact, even more specifically, it's the Nantais region within the western, coastal part of the Loire Valley. Here then is a tour of the key styles that can be found there:

Muscadet 1: Generic, straight *'Muscadet'* can be made from grapes all over the three sub-appellations of the *Nantais* mentioned below. In general, these wines can seem a tad dilute, neutral and anaemic. In my humble opinion, it would be well worth paying just a little bit more for any of the following:

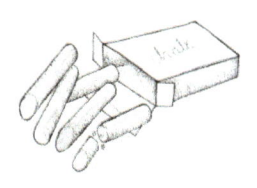

Muscadet 2: *Muscadet Sèvre-et-Maine*. Responsible for over 75% of Muscadet production, this is the best-known sub-appellation and should offer a step-up in quality. Wines can be a little hit and miss in reality, though.

Muscadet 3&4: *Muscadet Coteaux de la Loire* and *Muscadet Côtes de Grandlieu* make up around 20% of production and can be a touch more flowery and salty.

Muscadet 5: The style that's generally considered to be the best is Muscadet *'Sur Lie'*. These are wines that have been kept for up to 12 months on their 'lees' (the dead yeast cells left over from the fermentation process). This *Sur Lie* (literally, *On Lees*) production style gives wines that are fuller bodied with extra texture and character. It also gives Muscadet that characteristic prickle of CO_2 so no, that slight fizz is not a fault! A Muscadet *Sur Lie* is well worth trading up for.

Red Grape Vinalogies

CABERNET SAUVIGNON

VINALOGY: The Professional Rugby Player

You can generally presume that all professional rugby players have certain elements in common: they are **full in body**, fairly **heavy** and particularly **well structured**. There are forwards who pack a slightly bigger punch, and backs who are a tad more refined and lean, but generally speaking, you can always tell a rugby player a mile off, no matter where in the team they play. It's the obvious build and all those **purpley-black** bruises that do it! And with all their years of training and experience, you can take a bet that their playing **quality** is going to be **pretty reliable**, no matter which country it is that they play for. They also tend to **need a few years to chill out** and learn how to behave...

Yes, Cabernet Sauvignon is the professional rugby player of the wine world! This heavy-duty grape variety has the thickest skin of all the grapes, giving it lots of tannin* and plenty of brawn! 'Cabernet', as it's often known, is a hardy, well-structured grape that makes pretty reliable wine just about anywhere. This is why you can find it all over the world now. When at its very best, it can take a few years to mature and mellow, so bear that in mind when you're picking one out. Look for a concentrated, dark blue-black and purple colour with distinctive, spicy blackcurrant and cedar flavours. In some cases, you'll also spot a telltale minty or eucalyptus note, which is often a hint that it's from a warmer climate.

FACT: Cabernet is so hardy and totally international that it's known as a 'noble' grape. The fine, über expensive wines of Bordeaux's left bank, such as the famous Château Margaux are Cabernet dominated, yet you can also buy a Chilean bottle of Cab for around £5...

* What's tannin? See Wine FAQ in **Chapter 5**.

Cabernet Sauvignon is...
- Opaque purple in colour
- Full bodied with lots of tannin
- All about blackcurrant, cedar and, sometimes, mint
- Star grape of Bordeaux's Left Bank, but famous worldwide

CABERNET SAUVIGNON TASTING TOUR

Cabernet 1: Be prepared to spend some cash and head to *Bordeaux, France*: the old world home of Cabernet, where it's usually blended* with Merlot among other grapes. Look for one from the *Left Bank* of the river Gironde for a classic earthy, cedary number that's Cabernet dominant.

Cabernet 2: Compare your Bordeaux with a Cabernet from *Coonawarra* in *Australia* for a fuller-bodied, juicier version with tonnes of blackcurrant and a characteristic minty twang.

Cabernet 3 & 4: At a similar price to Bordeaux, you could also try some serious Cabs from *Napa Valley, California* or *Washington State* for big wines made in a Bordeaux blend* style but with a pleasing extra dab of fruit.

Cabernets 6+: For something a little more entry-level price wise, check out what they can do with Cabernet over in *Chile, Eastern Europe* and *South Africa*.

* What's a blend? See Wine FAQ in **Chapter 5**.

PINOT NOIR

VINALOGY: The Ballerina

When I was younger, I wanted to be a ballerina: **elegant** and **pale skinned,** they were femininity personified in my eyes and I would often imagine myself as one in a **silky**, **cherry**-red tutu, floating gracefully across the stage in a waft of **lavender**-scented mist. Sure, they're notoriously **temperamental**, and many people also find them too **thin**, but I have always been mesmerised by their haunting beauty and ability to make complex moves seem so smooth and effortless. It is all of these qualities, the good and the bad, that make the ballerina a perfect Vinalogy for Pinot Noir.

Pinot is famously difficult to work with, which is why there are so many disappointing offerings on the market. When all conditions are perfect and the masters get hold of it, however; oh man. You'll want to bathe in the stuff! Pale in colour, light bodied and elegant, with high acidity and very low tannin, Pinot can taste like a red wine but feel like a white, which is part of its universal charm. Couple this with a sensual, silky texture and an ethereal perfume of spiced cherry, lavender, raspberry compote and earth, and you'll understand why people spend crazy amounts on the top bottles!

FACT: Pinot Noir is one of the three main grapes used in Champagne, along with Chardonnay and the lesser-known Pinot Meunier. If you have a 'Blancs de Noir' Champagne, it has been made with the red grapes only: usually Pinot Noir and often with a touch of Pinot Meunier.

FACT: If it's red and the label says 'Bourgogne' (French for 'Burgundy'), it's going to be Pinot Noir, even if it doesn't say so.

TIP: Find a cool-climate Pinot that's a few years old. That's where the magic happens and you get those seductive, earthy flavours.

Pinot Noir is...
- Very pale, morello cherry red
- Light bodied and elegant
- All about spiced cherry compote, lavender and earth
- Star red grape of Burgundy, France, but famous worldwide

PINOT NOIR TASTING TOUR

Pinot Noir 1: You can't do Pinot Noir without heading to *Burgundy, France*. Top-end red Burgundies are best with a few years of age on them. Think spicy cherry and lavender flavours with a marzipan note. They're delicate, earthy, understated and old school in style, but also often rather expensive!

Pinot Noir 2: *New Zealand* is one of the ultimate destinations for great New World Pinot; it's easy drinking, yet serious. The savoury red fruit and cinnamon notes in wines from this country have won hearts and palates worldwide.

Pinot Noir 3 & 4: The fog-cooled parts of coastal *California* give their Pinots softness, while that ripe, juicy fruit still shines through. They're all about strawberries and cream on a bed of red velvet. *Oregon* Pinots are well worth trying too. They lean more towards a Burgundian style thanks to the cooler climate up there.

Pinot Noir 5: *Chilean* Pinot is often fuller bodied and more savoury-smoky than other versions, not to mention inexpensive. Come here for something spicy with bright damson and raspberry fruit flavours.

63

MERLOT

VINALOGY: The Easy Listening Grape

♪♪ *I love Merlot in the springtime…* ♪♪

You can't go wrong with a bit of **easy listening** at a party. Stick it on and let the **smooth**, **chocolatey** tones wash over you. The sound is as familiar and **uncomplicated** as your comfiest pyjamas. Sure, it may have become a bit of a cliché, and many don't want to admit having it in their collection, but the formula works and the style is easy enough for anyone to like. And although much of the time it is mere background music, every so often there's a 'My Way' and you can't help but sing along!

Merlot is the easy-drinking, medium-bodied, smooth and low-tannin grape that's a great choice for crowd pleasing in any situation. It's typically bright red and soft with flavours of juicy tomato, milk chocolate and sometimes – a bit weirdly – a metallic tang that might remind you of blood! In a good way. Sometimes.

Despite some bad press in recent years, like certain crooning front men we all know and love, Merlot sales are increasing again. It usually makes wine that's pretty uncomplicated, but just occasionally a 'My Way' Merlot will be produced with more cedar and tobacco flavours. Ever heard of Château Pétrus in Bordeaux, for example? With nearly 100% Merlot, Pétrus is arguably one of the finest wines on the planet!

FACT: The Cheval Blanc 1961 that the Merlot-hating Miles drinks at the end of the film, SIDEWAYS, is actually a blend of Merlot and Cabernet Franc from Bordeaux. The bad Merlots he was referring to were the cheap, sugary versions made in his part of the world.

> **Merlot is…**
> - Bright red in colour
> - Super soft and juicy
> - All about ripe tomato, milk chocolate and, sometimes, blood
> - The star grape of Bordeaux's Right Bank but famous worldwide

MERLOT TASTING TOUR

Merlot 1: Merlot's European home is firmly in *Bordeaux* and, more specifically, *St-Emilion* and *Pomerol* on the right bank of Bordeaux's River Gironde. It's rare to find wines that are 100% Merlot, as other grapes such as Cabernet Franc and Cabernet Sauvignon are often added as seasoning, but many are nearly there. Save your pennies for this original, tobacco-spiced Merlot experience!

Merlot 2 & 3: Next, head to *Australia* or *Chile* for soft and juicy versions that pack a little more punch thanks to all that extra sunshine! You may find also find a spicy, textured note from oak ageing in these wines.

Merlot 4: For a step-up in serious elegance, head to *Hawke's Bay* in *New Zealand* where some beautiful, classy Merlots are now being produced in a Bordeaux style with a herbal, earthy character.

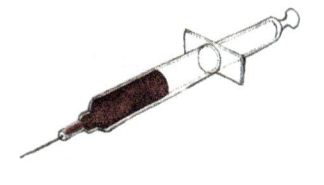

Merlot 4: If it's inexpensive Merlot you're after, however, try with a few Northern *Italian* Merlots from regions like the *Veneto* and *Friuli*. These are the easy-drinking, soft, red-fruited kind of style.

SYRAH (aka SHIRAZ)

VINALOGY: Shakespeare Vs Pantomime

"Come, Sirrah. Crush a cup of wine!"

Intricately laced corsets or gaudy, purple wigs; which do you fancy today? Sometimes you want substance when you go to the theatre; the complex words, twists and turns of a Shakespeare play, for example. Other times however, a light-hearted pantomime is what's called for, complete with colourful hairdos, singing and slapstick! It's a matter of taste, and both styles can be perfectly executed, though they couldn't be more different.

69

Syrah and Shiraz are the same grape variety; one is just the alter ego of the other, where the name used refers to the final *style* of the wine. France's Rhône Valley is the original home of Syrah, where the grape shows off a feast of Shakespearian proportions! Think **savoury** flavours of **grilled meat**, **thyme**, **white pepper** and **violets**.

Shiraz on the other hand, is more Panto than Prospero: **full-on**, **purple** and **ripe**, with flavours of **plum jam** and **liquorice spice**. Shiraz is traditionally a lot **fruitier** than its alter ego, Syrah. It has been synonymous with warmer, New World climates, whereas Syrah is firmly an Old World, European style. Nowadays, however, you'll find some serious New World Syrahs, so named because they capture some of that Rhône-ish, **savoury violet** vibe. All hail the 'Rhône Rangers'!

FACT: Syrah is one of the three key grape varieties used in the famous blends of Châteauneuf-du-Pape: a production area (appellation) in France's Southern Rhône Valley. Syrah is also the flagship red grape for most of the reds in the Northern Rhône Valley where the wines are named after the villages rather than the grapes.

Syrah is...
- Deep purple in colour
- Full bodied but not overly tannic
- All about violets, plums and dried herbs
- The star grape of the Rhône Valley, France

Shiraz is...
- Deep purple in colour
- Full bodied but not overly tannic
- All about spicy plum jam, liquorice and white pepper
- The star grape of the Barossa Valley, Australia

SYRAH (aka SHIRAZ) TASTING TOUR

Syrah 1: Spilt the Rhône Valley in two and head North to the production areas of *Saint-Joseph*, *Cornas*, *Hermitage* and *Crozes-Hermitage* for quintessential *Rhône* Syrah that's famous for savoury, smoked meat and violet-scented deliciousness.

Syrah 2+: For a Syrah style with an extra veneer of silky, new world charm, try some wines from *Hawke's Bay* in *New Zealand*, *Chile's Elqui or Limari Valleys*, *California* or *Washington State*. 'Syraz'?

***

Shiraz 1: For exemplary Shiraz, *Australia,* especially the *Barossa Valley,* is the place to head for liquorice sticks and that generous, spiced damson and juicy, jam fix.

Shiraz 2: Coming at it another way, *Mendoza* in *Argentina* is producing some really classy versions of Shiraz. Think Panto, but immaculately performed by London's National Theatre! 'Shirah'? I'll get my coat...

MALBEC

VINALOGY: The Polo Player

The barbecue is fired up and it's not just the steaks that are sizzling. As the aroma of **grilled steak** fills the air in that sunny, open field, you spot them on the sidelines before the match: the beautiful people, the polo players.

Mr and Mrs Malbec are **smooth** seduction in a bottle. Wearing **distinctive**, **raspberry**-pink team shirts that only their kind can get away with, they're **toned** and **athletic** rather than rugby-player chunky, with lustrous, **silky** hair that you can't help but want to stroke. One of them looks at you, **intense** and **concentrated**, with **cocoa**-coloured eyes framed by **soft**, long lashes. A rogue polo ball has left a **blueberry**-coloured bruise on their cheek.

***

Yes, Malbec certainly grabs the attention. There are not many grapes that you can recognise in the glass just by looking at them, but Malbec is one: concentrated to the point of being opaque, with bright, raspberry-pink tears that will drip down your glass. With a lean and firm structure, Malbec will seduce you with silky tannins, fresh blueberry tones, a touch of grilled meat and a soft flourish of chocolate.

Park that polo pony and let's get stuck in!

FACT: Malbec the grape is actually French in origin, but it has done so well in its adopted home of Argentina that it is now considered the country's flagship red grape variety.

FACT: Malbec has lots of complicated French synonyms from 'Pressac' to 'Auxerrois', 'Côt' to 'Jacobain'.

> **Malbec is...**
> - Opaque and dark magenta, often with tell-tale pink 'legs'*
> - Full bodied but velvety smooth
> - All about chocolate-dipped raspberries and blueberries
> - The star red grape of Argentina

* What are 'legs'? See Wine FAQ Chapter 5

MALBEC TASTING TOUR

Malbec 1: For a classic, polo-playing Malbec experience with chocolate-dipped raspberry flavours, head straight to *Mendoza* or *Patagonia* in *Argentina*.

Malbec 2: Stay in *Mendoza*, *Argentina*, but throw a little more money at something that boasts a vineyard with a particularly high altitude: anything over 1,500m above sea level if you can! You'll find that your Malbec takes on an incredible intensity of flavour, ramping up the blueberry and adding, somehow, the sweet scent of fresh, clean air. Just, wow!

Malbec 3: Next, head to *Cahors* in *South West France* for some inky black wines rich in mulberry spice. 'Cahors' will be Malbec dominant, although here, they usually refer to it as 'Auxerrois'.

Malbec 4: For something quite different and lighter in style, head to *France's Loire Valley* and look for a wine made from 'Côt'. Here, it's often blended with Cabernet Franc or Gamay.

PINOTAGE

VINALOGY: The Rock Star

There's a formula to the true rock star: a **smoke-tinged**, gravelly voice that intoxicates in seconds and a **big**, **brooding** personality that has **dark**, dark days. Moments of glory are followed by downright scary displays of behaviour, from looking like they've been dragged through a **bramble bush** backwards, to the smell of **burning rubber** as the publicist's car whisks them away!

Unique, **sultry** and **unpredictable**, you're never quite sure what you're going to get, but you'll forgive them anything, for around the corner is a producer that'll coax out the very best of what they can do.

***

Pinotage is South Africa's signature red grape and is constantly fighting a bad-ass reputation. It's the grape with a big personality that expresses itself boldly, often rubbing people up the wrong way. In the right producer's hands, however, it's capable of making delicious wines packed full of dark, brambly fruit. For years, it has suffered with smoke addiction, showcasing distinctive and unsubtle burnt rubber and bonfire aromas, but scratch the surface and you'll find buckets of blackberries and earthy, green olive flavours. When a producer has tamed it, cutting the smoke and upping the freshness, then wow! It is just what you need to warm the cockles. Styles tend to vary according to producer more than anything else, so get to know them a little better if you can.

FACT: Pinotage is so named because it was developed from crossing the *Pinot* Noir grape variety with the Hermi*tage* grape (now known as Cinsault). Hence *Pino-tage*.

Pinotage is...
- Dark, purpley red in colour
- Often high in alcohol and body but not very tannic
- All about bonfires and barbecues with brambly fruit
- The star red grape of South Africa

PINOTAGE TASTING TOUR

There's not much going on with Pinotage outside South Africa yet, so my tip is to experiment with the various producers until you find one who makes a style you like. A few particularly good names to look out for are Fairview, Kanonkop, Simonsig, Groot Constantia and Beyerskloof.

Pinotage 1: The *Stellenbosch* region of *South Africa* is where you'll find classic examples of Pinotage, but other areas such as *Paarl* are also worth trying!

Pinotage 2+: While South Africa really is the place for Pinotage, there are a few experiments going on elsewhere. If you can find them, try some wines from *New Zealand* and *California*.

TEMPRANILLO

VINALOGY: The Mysterious Cowboy

In the early hours of morning you hear a noise, and then you spot him from your window. He's back: the mysterious cowboy. The man is a legend in these parts and each town has a **different name** for him. You watch this figure oozing **masculinity** and allure in faded **leather** boots as he unsaddles his horse. You spoke to him once: his voice was **soft** as velvet and sweet, like **wild strawberry**. He smelled of **wood smoke** mingled with fresh, **vanilla tobacco**. It has been a long time. He has **aged well**.

Introducing Tempranillo: the mysterious cowboy of the wine world. This ruggedly handsome and early-ripening grape ('temprano' is Spanish for 'early') is all male with its savoury character. The flavours of leathery, cinnamon spice that temper wild strawberry notions are often exacerbated by years of ageing in oak barrels. The result is a mellow, spicy wine that's moreishly chewy. Think of comfortable, worn leather, tobacco, liquorice and stewed strawberry fruit.

FACT: Tempranillo is Spain's flagship red grape, although you may not realise it given the many aliases it has. Known as 'Tempranillo' in the famous *Rioja* region where it's the principal grape used in the red wines, our cowboy is also known as Cencibel, Ull de Llebre, Tinta de Pais, Tinta de Toro, Tinto de Madrid.... Tinto de wherever-it's from, and that's just Spain!

Tempranillo is...
- Bright, strawberry red in colour
- Soft and very juicy
- All about wild strawberry, worn leather and liquorice
- The star grape of Rioja, Spain

TEMPRANILLO TASTING TOUR

Tempranillo 1: When you think of Tempranillo, your first thought should be Spain. Head straight to the region of *Rioja* and start with the younger versions before working your way up the age ladder: go from *Joven* (meaning 'young' in Spanish) to *Crianza*, then *Reserva* and, finally, *Gran Reserva*. The difference is the amount of time the wine has aged in oak and then in bottle before release. Both bottle and oak age increase as you move up the scale.

Tempranillo 2: Stay in Spain, but mosey on over to *Ribera del Duero*: an exciting area for Tempranillo where wines traditionally have more body and power than those from Rioja thanks to slightly different geography.

Tempranillo 3: In *Portugal's Douro*, Tempranillo is known as Tinta Roriz. It's one of the principal blending grapes in Port, but is now also making some stunning, still, dry wines that simply must be tasted.

Tempranillo 4+: Various regions in *Australia* are now producing some delicious, juicy, red-fruited Tempranillo from the *Margaret River* region in the West all the way over to the *Barossa Valley* in the East. There is also some exciting experimentation going on in the *USA*. *Oregon* and *California* in particular are turning out wines of particularly high quality.

SANGIOVESE

VINALOGY: The Perfect Tuscan Family

I've always loved Italians: they do the family thing so well! When I think of Italy's Sangiovese grape, I think of a picture-perfect Tuscan family: model parents and two strapping sons.

Morellino, the mother, is a forward little thing and as bright as a button. She is gentle, approachable and always up and ready to go before her boys. As the only lady in the house, she's often ignored as the lads jostle for attention.

Chianti, the youngest boy, has just started school. Unruly at times, he can be very good or very, very bad. He's a rustic country boy that needs a good meal to soften his edges.

Chianti Classico is the older brother: straight down the line and well behaved, he is the model student, displaying characteristics that his parents would be proud of.

Brunello is the daddy of the Sangiovese family and comes from high society stock based in a different town. He is more tanned and broad shouldered than his Chianti boys will ever be and there are many layers to his personality. It takes time to get to know him.

TIP: Try 'Riserva' versions of all of these for more dark spice and complexity that come from longer ageing in oak.

***

NOTE: A brand new classification has been announced as I write. 'Gran Selezione' wine will rank above Chianti Classico Riserva in terms of quality.

In Chianti, the grape's called 'Sangiovese' (meaning blood of Jove), but on the Tuscan coast, it becomes 'Morellino'. Inland, around the town of Montalcino, it has a beefier clone known as 'Brunello' and in Corsica, it's 'Nielluccio', but it's all the same family with subtle differences depending on location. Their common features, however, are **earthy**, **savoury cherry** and **dried herb** flavours that go deliciously with local Italian food.

> **Sangiovese is...**
> - Deep red with brownish tinges
> - Tangy and high in acidity: great with Italian food
> - All about savoury cherry, dried herbs and earth
> - The star red grape of Tuscany, Italy

SANGIOVESE TASTING TOUR

Sangiovese 1: *Morellino di Scansano* – From *Tuscany's Western Coast*, *Morellino* is approachable and soft, with bright red fruit and made for earlier drinking. Lesser known, but one to watch!

Sangiovese 2: *Chianti* – Rustic, with sour cherry and dried herb flavours. Grapes are picked in various locations all over the Tuscan *Chianti* production zone.

Sangiovese 3: *Chianti Classico* – Richer, darker cherry notes with cocoa bean and dried herbs. They're from the very best *'classic' zone* within the Chianti region.

Sangiovese 4: *Brunello di Montalcino* - Sangiovese with a six-pack! This chunky clone of the grape from the Tuscan town of *Montalcino* is fuller bodied and earthy, showing off mineral, violet, leather and tobacco flavours.

Sangiovese 5: *Vino Nobile di Montepulciano* - The posh country cousin of Chianti. It's Sangiovese from the nearby town of *Montepulciano* made with a dusty, old school approach. (Note: Don't confuse it with Montepulciano d'Abruzzo; Montepulciano is a different grape variety!)

Sangiovese 6+: Italy is the real home of Sangiovese, but some relations have flown the nest! Look for them in small pockets around *Australia*, *Argentina* and *California*: all with those unmistakable Italian looks, but defined accents from their own country.

ZINFANDEL

VINALOGY: The Hollywood Icon

Fancy a night in with a Hollywood **Icon**? Well, who would be your leading man? Someone enigmatic and **bold** who **demands attention**? Throw in a penchant for **alcohol**, a tendency to put on **weight** and an intriguing **European heritage**, and there could be several contenders. If that's who you're after then it has got to be Zinfandel: the Hollywood Icon of the grape varieties, the Godfather of wine!

89

Full-on, **full bodied** and frequently **high in alcohol**, 'Zin' is not exactly a subtle wine. It oozes **black cherry jam, prune** and **spicy fig** flavours together with a fair whack of **tannin** that'll stain your teeth bright blue. With roots in Europe (it has been genetically linked to Italy's Primitivo and Croatia's Crljenak Kastelanski grapes), the Californian treatment has made Zin a star and there's no ignoring this captivating wine! So, if you're a fan of big, charismatic personalities, Zinfandel is the way to go.

TIP: Look for 'Old Vines' on the label. Old vines produce fewer grapes and therefore make the wine much more concentrated and rustic.

FACT: 'White Zinfandel' is, confusingly, actually a pink or 'blush' wine. It's made from the exact same red Zinfandel grape, so could really be called 'Zinfandel rosé'.

Zinfandel is…
- Dark purple and opaque with big, fat legs
- Full-on and full bodied
- All about figs, prunes and black cherry jam
- The star grape of California, USA

ZINFANDEL TASTING TOUR

Get some food on your plate and head straight to California to compare the key regional styles:

Zinfandel 1: *Dry Creek Valley* in *Sonoma* produces the oldest vines and dark, peppery styles.

Zinfandel 2: *Napa Valley* Zinfandel tends to show more of a juicy, exuberant, bright berry style.

Zinfandel 3: Next, head to the *Sierra Foothills* for inky-black aniseed and mineral flavours...

Zinfandel 4: ...or try *Lodi* and *Paso Robles* for more herbal, ripe cherry notes.

Zinfandel 5: *Russian River Valley*, the *Santa Cruz Mountains* and *Mendocino County* are relatively cool in comparison, so produced quite an elegant, less alcoholic and more complex style of Zinfandel.

Zinfandel 6: Zinfandel has its roots in Europe and is genetically very similar to the Italian *Primitivo* grape variety, so once you've hit California, head on to *Puglia* in *Southern Italy* for a more rustic and restrained European version.

Zinfandel 7+: Other than California and Italy, you'll be hard pressed to find Zin anywhere else. *South Africa* and *Western Australia*, however, have recently had a small amount of success with it.

NEBBIOLO

VINALOGY: The Ladyboy

You are standing in a dingy Milanese club, drink in hand, waiting for the show to start. The lights go down and the stage fills with **fog**. A figure steps forward into the spotlight. A woman. You think you recognise her; the **slim body**, the elegance, the **pale** skin. She has the figure of a ballerina at first glance, but no. There's something different. You can't quite put your finger on it.

After her set, you approach her. Her perfume is seductive: **violets** and **rose petals**, but with undertones of something darker. **Liquorice? Tar?** She speaks. You expect French, but her accent is Italian. Local. Still, there's something different. You get talking. You take her home. You go upstairs. You slowly undress her, and then wham! You discover that something different... This grape has **balls**! It's the ladyboy of Piedmont!

***

Nebbiolo can look as graceful and feminine as a Pinot Noir, but once you get it in your mouth, there's no comparison. It's all male! Nebbiolo is an intriguing paradox, especially with a bit of age on it because it's pale, perfumed and delicate in appearance and aroma, but is full bodied, has high acidity and lots of tooth-drying tannin once you get it in your mouth. It makes wine that can go on for years and not lose power. Think roses and violets, marzipan, tar and truffles. Curious? Give the ladyboy a go! I won't tell...

FACT: Nebbiolo is named after the rolling **fog** (*nebbia*) of the Piedmont region in Northern Italy where this grape is king. The greatest examples of Nebbiolo make the famous Italian wines of *Barolo* and *Barbaresco*.

Nebbiolo is...
- Pale violet, quite like a Pinot
- Hugely tannic, belying its looks!
- All about rose petals, marzipan, tar and truffles
- The star red grape of Piedmont, Italy

NEBBIOLO TASTING TOUR

Nebbiolo is a homebody. It doesn't like leaving the apron strings of Northern Italy, although increasingly other countries are experimenting. Get to know your ladyboy a little better with a few examples from the following places:

Nebbiolo 1: *Barolo*, *Barbaresco* and *Gattinara* are the big boys from *Piedmont*, *Northern Italy* and are what the best Nebbiolos (Nebbioli?) are all about! Both are much better with a few years' age on them, so save your pennies and throw some cash at a decent, aged bottle. It'll be worth it.

Nebbiolo 2: Compare the Piedmont big boys with a fresh-faced, wallet-friendly *Nebbiolo d'Alba* (meaning literally 'Nebbiolo from Alba'), again, from within *Piedmont*. These tend to be softer, more approachable and you drink them much earlier. They won't have the intensity and character of Barolo and Barbaresco, but sometimes, you want it easy.

Nebbiolo 3: Some interesting examples are now coming out of *Oregon* and *Washington State* where they are getting closer to the Italian style. Your main issue, however, could be trying to get hold of them in Europe.

Nebbiolo 4+: The *Margaret River* region in *Western Australia* is producing some lovely Nebbiolo in a more juicy style, and some winemakers in *Victoria* are starting to have success too.

Chapter 3

START SPEAKING WINE LANGUAGE

"It's thin, smells of dead leaves and tastes of cow poo. In a good way."

These were the only words I could find to describe a stunning, bottle-aged, Burgundian Pinot Noir the first time I tried one. It was also the exact moment I realised that wine is a language that needs to be learned just like any other. It just happens to be the most exasperating language you'll ever find because you can recognise all the words in the sentence, yet still not understand a thing!

It takes time and dedication to learn wine language and you won't be fluent immediately, but here's how you make a start:

* *Pay attention* to what you're drinking

It sounds obvious, but step one is simply to start paying attention. Think about it; if you've been driving since you were seventeen and you're now thirty, how much have you actually improved in the last ten years? Driving on autopilot, are you? Probably. Well, it's the same with wine; you may have been drinking the stuff for years but have you ever stopped to try to put what you're tasting into words?

* Taste by *comparison*

I always show several wines at once at my tastings because it's by comparing and contrasting wines that the differences between them in terms of aroma, flavour and texture really pop out. See **Chapter 6** for some comparative tasting ideas.

* Find your *own words*

At first, your notes will probably go: 'looks like wine, smells like wine, tastes like wine'. Keep going, however, taste by comparison and you'll eventually start picking out anything from 'cat pee' to 'weird herbal sausages'. Don't worry if it sounds a bit bonkers in the beginning; any descriptor is a good thing! Make notes.

* *Translate* your own words into winespeak

Once you have some of your own words, compare them with what the pros say on the back of bottles or on wine lists. You'll soon start noticing that the same descriptors come up time and again for certain grapes and wine styles. My 'thin, dead leaves and cow poo-in-a-good-way' eventually became 'light bodied, with autumnal notes and a moreish hint of barnyard', but it took a while. And remember: describing wine is subjective, so don't ever feel that you've got it wrong. If you think it smells of feet, IT SMELLS OF FEET! It's just a wine pro's job to turn that description into something you might actually want to drink.

Chapter 4

UNDERSTANDING A WINE LIST

As with speaking and writing wine language, learning to decipher a wine list is a process. Here are some key things you need to know for a list to start making sense:

* GRAPES
If you know which grapes you like, you're halfway there, so get a feel for the major varieties (you saw that one coming, didn't you?) Maybe you're a fan of the buttery tones of a Chardonnay for example, or perhaps you prefer the fresh grassiness of a Sauvignon Blanc? The twenty Vinalogies in this book are a good place to start.

* THE SUNSHINE EFFECT
Remember that lots of sun equals fuller-bodied, juicier, fruitier and, generally, more alcoholic versions of that very same grape variety grown somewhere cooler. Country and region will therefore give you a huge hint about the final style of the wine.

* REGIONS
Very important this one: know that most wine regions, especially those in Europe, are synonymous with certain grape varieties. This is vital because in Europe (and France particularly), most wines are named after the place they come from – and sometimes the style – rather than the grapes used. Place or style is therefore what you'll usually see written on the label and therefore the wine list, so get to know the famous ones. White Sancerre will always be Sauvignon Blanc for example, and Chablis will always be Chardonnay. Red Burgundy is synonymous with Pinot Noir and red Rioja is mostly Tempranillo. My 'Tasting Tours' at the end of each Vinalogy will help you with this as will 'Wine Top Trumps' in **Chapter 7**.

* VOCAB LESSON

To understand a little more about the nuances of wine, get to know the meaning of some key terms that you'll find on labels. Here's a list of terms that I think you're most likely to need to know when it comes to still, sparkling and sweet wines and why they're important:

STILL WINE
Need-to-know terms and styles

FRENCH

Millésime – Vintage: the year written on the label (the year when the grapes were harvested).

Domaine – A wine estate; usually smaller than a 'château'.

Vieilles Vignes – 'Old vines'. Good because older vines produce fewer grapes and have deeper roots, which means more concentrated and complex wines.

Supérieur – Wine with higher (superior) alcohol content as a result of being made from riper grapes.

Cuvée – A cuvée simply refers to a specific blend or batch. From the French word 'cuve' meaning tank or vat.

Grand Cru – The top quality classification in Burgundy and Alsace. Also used in St-Emilion, Bordeaux, but its quality status is more ordinary there.

Premier Cru – The second highest quality level in Burgundy and Alsace.

Premier Cru Classé – The top quality classification on the Left Bank of Bordeaux. After that, you have the Deuxième Cru (2nd growth) etc. down to 5th Growth.

Premier Grand Cru Classé – The top quality classification on the Right Bank of Bordeaux. Split into A & B groups.

Grand Cru Classé – The second highest quality level on the Right Bank of Bordeaux.

GERMAN

Trocken – Dry or almost dry.

Feinherb – Just off-dry, though it's not a legally defined term!

Halbtrocken – Off-dry.

Lieblich – More of a medium style.

Pradikat – Superior quality wine.

Qualitätswein bestimmter Anbaugebiete (QbA) – Quality wine from a specific region.

Qualitätswein mit Prädikat (QmP) – Superior quality wine with 'specific attributes'.

Kabinett – Usually a light style of wine with low-ish alcohol.

Spätlese – A style that's more concentrated and highly flavoured than Kabinett. Sometimes sweeter, but not always. Made from riper grapes that have been picked late.

Auslese – A step up from Spätlese in terms of concentration and intensity. These wines can be sweet or dry, but usually sweet. Made with specifically selected, very ripe grape bunches.

SPANISH

Añejo – A wine that has been aged for at least three years, either in bottle or cask or both.

Cosecha – vintage or harvest.

Licoroso (Sp.) / Liquoroso (It.) – Sweet, fortified wine.

Pago – District or specifically named vineyard.

Joven – 'Young'. A wine that's usually un-oaked and made to be drunk soon.

Crianza – An aged wine. With Spanish reds, the wine must have been aged for at least 24 months in bottle or oak casks. At least 12 of these should be in oak. For white and pink wines to be called 'crianza', they must be aged for a minimum of 12 months with at least six months in oak.

Reserva – With Spanish reds, the wine must have been aged for at least 36 months in bottle or oak casks. At least 12 of these should be in oak. For white and pink wines to be called 'crianza', they must be aged for a minimum of 24 months with at least six months in oak. Outside of Spain, 'reserva' is a generic term that is supposed to denote a higher quality or an aged wine, but it's not regulated.

Gran Reserva – With Spanish reds, the wine must have been aged for at least 24 months in oak casks and then at least another 36 months in bottle. For white and pink wines to be called 'Gran Reserva', they must be aged for a minimum of 48 months, at least six months of which must be in oak.

Roble – 'Wood'. The wine has seen oak.

Rama / En Rama – A wine that has not been filtered or fined.

Rosado – Rosé or pink wine.

Tinto – Red wine

Viejo – Spanish term meaning 'old' and referring to a quality wine that undergoes a minimum period of ageing lasting three years.

ITALIAN

Abboccato – Medium-dry

Amabile – Semi-sweet

Annata – The year the grapes were harvested (the vintage year).

Azienda Agricola – Wine estate that uses its own grapes to produce its wines.

Bianco – White (wine)

Classico – From the central (and usually oldest) part of a production area.

Riserva – Aged for a specified time before release.

Rosato – Rosé (wine)

Rosso – Red (wine)

Seco – Dry

Semidulce – Semi-sweet

SPARKLING WINE
Need-to-know terms and styles

Brut – Dry (used for sparkling wine).

Demi-Sec – Semi sweet (used for sparkling wine).

Traditional method / Méthode traditionnelle
Term for the process that produces the highest possible quality of sparkling wine. The fizz is created by a secondary fermentation, which takes place inside the bottle resulting in fine, enduring bubbles. Champagne is always made this way.

Tank Method / Charmat Method
Where bubbles are created under pressure in a large tank before being transferred to a bottle. Not as high quality as traditional method and much cheaper to produce. Prosecco is made like this.

Crémant
Term for sparkling wine made according to the traditional method in France, but outside the Champagne region.

Mousseaux
A sparkling wine made in France, outside the Champagne region. It can be made using any method.

Spumante
Italian term for a 'fully sparkling wine'.

Frizzante
Italian term for a 'lightly sparkling wine'.

Asti
A sweet and soft, lightly sparkling Italian wine made from the Moscato grape and hailing from the Italian province of Asti.

Franciacorta
Italian sparkling wine from Lombardy made using the traditional method and, predominantly, Chardonnay and Pinot Bianco grapes.

Sekt
German term for 'sparkling wine' produced mostly using the Charmat method and very occasionally, the traditional method.

Cava
Spanish term for a key style of sparkling wine, largely produced in Catalonia by the traditional method and using a blend of Spanish grapes.

Blanc de Blancs
A sparkling wine made with entirely white grapes. In Champagne, 'blanc de blancs' must be made from 100% Chardonnay.

Blanc de Noirs
A sparkling wine made with entirely black grapes. In Champagne, this means Pinot Noir and Pinot Meunier.

Moscato d'Asti
This sweet Italian, low-alcohol, sparkling wine is sweet because fermentation is stopped by chilling, followed by removal of yeasts to prevent further fermentation. Bubbles are added afterwards.

SWEET WINE
Need-to-know terms and styles

Doux (Fr.) / Dulce (Sp.) / Dolce (It.) – Sweet

Late Harvest/Vendage Tardive
Where grapes are left hanging on the vine much later than usual. They dehydrate, concentrating the sugars and developing chemical compounds that change the flavour. ***Famous places:*** Alsace, but made worldwide.

Noble Rot/Botrytis Cinerea/Botrytis
Like late harvest wine, but with an extra dimension! That dimension is a 'noble rot' (Latin: Botrytis Cinerea) that eats the sugars and dehydrates the grape, producing glycerol and leaving complex marzipan and honey flavoured compounds. The rot is brought on by foggy, damp conditions. If a label says 'Sélection de Grains Nobles', it's made with botrytised grapes. ***Famous places***: Sauternes (France), Tokaji (Hungary), Germany, Loire Valley (France), especially Coteaux du Layon.

Eiswein/Ice wine
Where grapes freeze on the vine and the ice crystals are removed resulting in the concentration of grape sugars. Noble rot should not be a feature here. ***Famous Places***: Germany and Canada.

Fortified wine
Where a grape spirit such as brandy is added part way through fermentation, stopping the process in its tracks. This leaves some unfermented sugar from the grape juice and adds a high alcohol kick from the brandy. ***Famous examples***: Port, sweet Sherry, Madeira, Marsala, Rutherglen Muscat (Australia) and the French 'Vins Doux Naturels' (VDNs) such as Muscat de Baumes de Venise, Banyuls and Maury.

Passito/Dried grape wines/Recioto ITALIAN
Here, grapes are picked and dried away from the vines to remove water and concentrate flavour. *Famous examples* include Vin Santo, Recioto di Soave and Recioto di Valpolicella.

Beerenauslese (BA) GERMAN
Rich and luscious, sweet dessert wine that can be kept for years. These are rare wines made with individually selected grapes that have been infected with botrytis (aka noble rot).

Trockenbeerenauslese (TBA) GERMAN
Like beerenauslese, but even sweeter and more intense! Again, made with noble rot and very rare.

Chapter 5

WINE FAQ
Answers to common wine questions

- What is 'tannin'? 109
- What does 'corked' mean? 110
- What is a 'vintage' wine? 110
- What are 'legs' and what do they signify? 111
- What is 'terroir'? 111
- What is a 'blend'? 111
- What do 'Old World' and 'New World' mean? 112
- Should you decant every wine? 113
- Why do waiters make you taste wine before serving? 113
- How long should you keep a wine before opening it? 113
- How long can you keep an open bottle of wine? 114
- Are Cabernet Sauvignon and Sauvignon Blanc related? 114
- How can wine taste like strawberry etc? 115
- Do plants grown near the vine affect flavour? 115
- Do wines really taste that different from each other? 115
- Is such poncy wine language really necessary? 116
- Are corks better than screw caps? 116
- Why does red wine give you a headache? 117

What is 'tannin'?
Swirl a big red wine around your mouth and swallow. Are you left with a chewy, dry feeling? Are you licking your teeth and gums? This substance is called 'tannin' and it's the same stuff that you find in over-stewed tea. With wine, however, it comes from the grape skins, stalks and, sometimes, the oak barrels, too. Some grape varieties have much thicker skins than others, and so will produce a lot more tannin. It's one way of telling the difference between grape types. See **Chapter 6** for some tasting experiments.

What does 'corked' mean?
When a wine is corked, it smells and/or tastes of musty old churches, damp cellars and mouldy sports kit, although very low levels of cork taint can just mute aromas and flavours. They call it 'corked' because traditionally, a chlorine-derived substance called TCA (full name: 2,4,6-Trichloroanisole) gets onto corks through less-than-perfect sterilisation processes and taints the wine in the bottle. It can happen to any wine closed with a cork, regardless of price. It can also happen to wines under screw caps, albeit it at a much lesser rate. What it does *not* mean, is that there are bits of cork floating in the bottle. That's just annoying.

What is a 'vintage' wine?
The 'vintage' is the year that the grapes were grown and, therefore, the year printed on the label. The vintage can be good or not so good, depending on the climatic conditions at the time the grapes were growing. We still tend to associate the term 'vintage' with very high quality, but most wines are technically 'vintage' these days, i.e. made from grapes grown in one particular year rather than a blend of several years. It doesn't necessarily mean that the vintage was a good one! One exception to this is Champagne, where they tend to only make 'vintage' wines in outstanding years.

Different regions may experience their growing seasons or 'vintages' very differently and there's much more variation from year to year in certain places. Bordeaux and Burgundy in France, for example, place a lot of importance on the vintage because their weather is so marginal; quality can therefore vary enormously from one year to the next. In places with much more even climates such as parts of Chile or Argentina, there's generally less variation from vintage to vintage.

Wines that are made from a blend of various years are described as Non-Vintage. This will be indicated by the letters NV on the label or simply by the lack of a year.

What are 'legs' and what do they signify?

'Legs', also known as 'tears' or 'church windows', are what you see dripping down the sides of your wine glass after you've given it a swirl. You won't see much with very light-bodied wines, whereas full-bodied and alcoholic wines will have fairly thick, viscous legs dripping down that glass. It's really just a sign that the wine is fairly high in alcohol, which can be explained by the fact that alcohol has a lower surface tension than water. They are not an indicator of quality so much as a sign that you are about to drink a big ol' boy.

What is 'terroir'?

'Terroir' is probably the ponciest wine word of them all and therefore definitely one to learn if you want to blend in with the pros! 'Terroir' refers to the specific combination of soil, topography and climate at any given vineyard site. Winemakers often talk about their wine being 'a great expression of the terroir' which basically means that the finished wines show nuances that can be attributed to the soil, climate and/or topography of that one, specific vineyard site where the grapes grew. It's what makes their wines unique.

What is a 'blend'?

In wine terms, a 'blend' means a mix of two or more grape varieties. Different grape types have different attributes; some are naturally very high or low in acidity for example, so blending can be a great way to balance a wine out as well as making it more interesting by adding layers of flavour. One of the most famous wine regions for producing blends is Bordeaux where the 'blended' result is much better than the individual grape components. Here's a *Vinalogy* to help: Think of that famous mint-with-a-hole. Well, Cabernet is the mint part, whereas Merlot is the hole: Cabernet has lots of tannin and the firm structure but can be a little austere alone, lacking a soft middle. Merlot on the other hand has plenty of soft, fruity 'middle', but often lacks the backbone and structure that makes a good wine great. Put the two together and you have the perfect team. They are the Fred and Ginger, the Batman and Robin, the Posh and Becks of the wine world! Other famous blends include *Châteauneuf-du-Pape* and *Sauternes*.

Winemakers often add tiny quantities of various grapes to increase flavour complexity, add colour, acidity, tannin etc, in the same way that we would add spice to a recipe. They're not the main ingredients, but can add the kick that makes the magic. If the amount used is very small (i.e. making up 15% or less of the total blend) you may not even see it written on the label.

What do 'Old World' and 'New World' mean?
The 'Old World' refers to wines from Europe essentially, where they have been making wine for centuries. The 'New World ' is precisely that: places like Australia, New Zealand, South America, South Africa and the USA where the winemaking industry is comparatively young. In very general terms, 'New World' wines are associated with warmer climates and younger vines so the wines tend to be fuller bodied, more fruity, more alcoholic and, generally, more in-your-face than their restrained, old-school, elegant, complex and sometimes austere 'Old World' cousins. 'New World' countries do have cooler regions where they make wines, but with practice you can usually still spot them in a line-up. It's that extra dollop of fruitiness that does it.

Should you decant every wine?
No. Decanting works well for heavier reds and particularly youthful wines. The point of decanting is to get oxygen into a wine, which opens up aroma, releases flavour and can soften harsh tannin a little. Some heavier whites can also benefit from being decanted. Lighter, more aromatic whites won't need it and very old reds may sometimes actually be better off staying in the bottle, as decanting may cause them to oxidise very quickly! Light to medium-bodied, everyday drinking reds won't benefit a huge amount from being decanted, but a pretty decanter does add a nice aesthetic touch to a dinner party. It also hides a crappy-looking bottle.

Why do waiters make you taste wine before serving?
They're asking you to check that the wine is not faulty, i.e. that it is not corked or oxidised (tasting vinegary or sherry-like), for example. It's *not* just for you to see if you like it. This can be tricky if you're not sure what you're looking for, but there's no shame in asking the waiter to check for you. If you have no idea what you're looking for but you like what you taste, then just go for it! Sometimes a restaurant may change a wine for you if you don't like it, even if it's not faulty, but that will be entirely at their discretion.

How long should you keep a wine before opening it?
It depends on the wine and the style that you like to drink. Are you into youthful, fresh fruit or do you prefer a leathery, cooked flavour? Young wines are all about primary fruit flavours, whereas older wines give you more layers of flavour and non-fruit notes like leather and caramel. As a rule of thumb, with everyday drinking wines, reds made with heavier grapes such as Cabernet Sauvignon will age for longer than lighter-bodied reds like Pinot Noir. Rosé and aromatic whites like Sauvignon Blanc

113

should usually be drunk straight away as their aromas and fruit will fade fairly quickly. Entry level-priced oak-aged whites will generally last for a year or two, but may not improve.

If the wine is a step or two up in quality from your average glug-glug: something red or white from Burgundy, Bordeaux or top-end Australia for example, they will usually benefit from a few years in the cellar. Again, it will depend on the exact wine in question so make sure you ask whoever sold it to you for their advice on that particular bottle or bottles, or check with someone in the know. Very generally, the more fruit flavour, acidity and tannin (if red) a wine has, the longer it will keep.

How long can you keep an open bottle of wine?
'Until you think it tastes bad' is the easiest answer here. An open bottle of wine may last around three days when kept in the fridge or up to a week if you use an anti oxidant wine-saving product. It really depends on your taste buds. It's not likely to make you ill even if it has been open for a couple of weeks.

Are Cabernet Sauvignon and Sauvignon Blanc related?
Cabernet Sauvignon is a *red* grape that makes full bodied red wine. Sauvignon Blanc is a *white* grape variety that makes particularly aromatic and distinctive white wines. Strangely enough, given their differences, the two are actually related! Cabernet Sauvignon is the 'son', or rather, the product of crossing the Cabernet Franc grape with Sauvignon Blanc, hence the name and therefore, the confusion. For all intents and purposes, however, they are two very different grape varieties that make wine styles that are poles apart.

How can wine taste like strawberry etc.?
Each grape variety has its own recognisable characteristics, and wine trade people learn to associate these with what they know in the outside world, be they fruit, flower, animal, mineral or vegetable. All grapes will vary slightly according to where they're grown and how they're made, but there will almost always be a signature aroma or flavour that screams 'I AM CABERNET!' or whichever grape it happens to be. This particular grape for example, has an unmistakable blackcurranty flavour. If it's particularly pronounced, juicy like Ribena and there's a minty note as well, then you can take a good guess that it comes from somewhere hot. Wines certainly don't taste of mint, strawberry or old leather because those things were mixed with the grape juice.

Do plants grown near the vine affect flavour?
Other plants grown in close proximity to the vines are generally not known to impart their specific flavours to the grapes. Having said that however, the jury may still be out; there are currently studies in Australia looking into whether the proximity of eucalyptus trees helps lend their characteristic note to wines as their oils become airborne and stick to the grape skins. *Soil* on the other hand almost certainly does help to give a certain texture to the wine. The soils of *Chablis* for example, give that characteristic dry, chalky texture to the Chardonnay there and the flinty soils of *Pouilly Fumé* often add a certain smokiness to the Sauvignon Blanc – hence the French word 'fumé' meaning smoked or smoky.

Do wines really taste that different from each other?
Absolutely – it just takes a bit of practice to notice the different flavours! You can even take a good guess at the grape variety just by looking at the wine's colour. And the more you know about wine, the more you get out of it.

People often ask why you'd ever need to spend more than £5 on a bottle of wine, but to me it's just like food; why cook a three-course meal for friends when a frozen pizza will do? Or buy a Jaguar XK when a Fiat Panda will also get you where you need to go? It's about the romance and pleasure of discovering flavours and all you need is a genuine interest and a bit of tasting practice.

Is such poncey wine language really necessary?
'Flowery' or 'poncey' wine language is used for more reasons than to simply differentiate between wines. In the wine trade, such intricate aroma, flavour and texture signifiers are necessary because they allow you to define a wine's quality and therefore, how much it should cost among other things. Is it typical for the area, for example? Does it taste as it should? Are all the elements in balance? Too much alcohol? Too little acid? You get the idea.

Are corks better than synthetic closures?
There are positives and negatives for all types of closure and experiments are constantly being done. Generally speaking though, when a cork is in perfect condition, it is still considered to be the ideal type of closure. As we all know, however, the number of corked bottles that greet the consumer is almost unforgivably high. Synthetic closures can still be tainted with TCA (See 'What is corked?') and therefore taste 'corked', but they are extremely rare. What they lack, however, is the sponginess and ability for oxygen exchange that cork has, which is what wine needs to age in the right way.

To sum up, screw caps are ideal for ready-to-drink, off-the-shelf wines, as the chance of spoilage is almost zero. Ditto with plastic corks, although they can be hard to get out, and look and feel cheap. If you want to keep a wine for a good few years, however, although modern screw caps may well be absolutely fine, a cork is still the preferred option. Just about.

Why does red wine give you headaches?
We all have different tolerances to things. Components of wine, such as sulphites, histamines, tannin and prostaglandin, contribute to pain and swelling and are released when wine is drunk. There are more of most of these elements in red wine compared with white, which is why some people feel the effects more with red. Another substance called Tyramine, which naturally occurs as food and drink age, can cause migranes. Red wines are generally more often associated with ageing, so this could be another reason for 'red-wine head'.

Chapter 6

TASTING WINE

Let's face it, when we're starting out, wine looks and smells like... well... wine. It's pretty difficult to form any clear notes on it. My advice is to start off by comparing two or three wines at once, because it's the *differences* between them all that will actually give you the answers. Once you've got a handle on the comparisons, it's much easier to then judge a single glass.

WHAT TO LOOK FOR WHEN YOU TASTE

Getting to know wine is not just about what it **tastes** like. Make sure you also pay attention to the following things as they are all clues about grape variety and, often, regional quirks. Taste your wine like a detective!

Colour: Ok, so a wine is red, but is it cherry red, brick red, or purple-red? Likewise, is a white wine pale lemon in colour, green-tinged or a rich yellow-gold? Make a note!

Concentration: Is it pale and watery or thick and opaque? Can you see straight through it or could you cut it with a knife?

Smell ('aroma'): Stick your nose right in the glass. Does the aroma jump out and slap you in the face or is there barely anything there? In winespeak, the first scenario is a 'pronounced' aroma and the latter is referred to as 'closed'.

Texture: Swill the wine all around your mouth, over your teeth and gums. You miss so much if you just glug it back! Pay attention to the way a wine *feels* in your mouth. Is it watery and tart ('acidic' in winespeak)? Does it have an oily texture? Does it feel heavy or light? Does it make you want to lick your teeth and gums (tannic)?

Flavour: Are you getting tart green fruit or ripe tropical fruit, for example? Crunchy red fruit like redcurrant, or dark purple fruit such as plum? Is the flavour pronounced or subtle? Are there lots of different complex flavours or is it one-dimensional like fruit cordial? Remember, tasting wine is subjective, so give it a taste descriptor – or Vinalogy - that *you're* not going to forget!

Aftertaste ('finish' or 'length'): Once you have swallowed the wine, breathe out. Can you still taste the flavour (a 'long finish') or does it disappear immediately ('short finish')? Is there an alcohol burn left in your throat? Does it leave a pleasant taste for example, or is it nasty and bitter?

Ideas for comparative wine tastings

Colour & Concentration
Some grape varieties have naturally thicker skins or skins that are naturally higher in pigment than others and so will produce more colour. Winemaking choices such as oak may add a tinge of caramel, but it will generally be enhancing what's already there. Make a note of colour, but also whether the wine is star bright or more opaque. Try to use un-oaked versions of grapes if you can and don't forget to swirl the glass to look at the 'legs' dripping down the glass!

Tasting ideas:

* Burgundian Pinot Noir Vs Chilean Merlot Vs Argentinian Malbec

* Any Sauvignon Blanc Vs New Zealand Chardonnay Vs Alsace Pinot Gris

Texture Tasting
Some grapes produce wines that have a higher natural *acidity* (more tart) than others. Some feel very *watery*, while others feel *thick* and *oily*. Some are *light bodied*, some *fuller bodied* and some have lots of *tannin*. Try these comparisons for size:

Tasting ideas:

* **Light Vs full bodied:**
French Pinot Noir Vs Australian Cabernet Sauvignon

* **Low Vs high tannin:**
New Zealand Pinot Noir Vs Australian Cabernet Sauvignon

* **High Vs low acidity:**
  Still, dry Loire Valley Chenin Blanc Vs Viognier

* **Watery & light Vs heavy & oily:**
  Loire Valley Sauvignon Blanc Vs Viognier

* **High Vs low alcohol:**
  French Pinot Noir Vs Californian Zinfandel

* **Chalky & mineral Vs soft & fruity:**
  Chablis Vs un-oaked Chilean or New Zealand Chardonnay

Regional Differences
Check out my Tasting Tours at the end of each Vinalogy for examples of the same grape grown in different wine regions around the world.

New World Vs Old World
This is essentially an experiment in climate. We're looking at Europe versus the likes of Australia, New Zealand and South America. The same grape variety will grow very differently all around the world and climate is often the key to the differences. Cool-climate wines tend to be more restrained, understated and elegant. Some call them 'old school' or even 'austere'; it depends on your taste! Wines from warmer places tend to be more obvious in aroma and flavour, with a fuller body, more fruit and more alcohol to boot. In very, very general terms, Old World wines are associated with the former style, and New World wines the latter. Try my Tasting Tours at the end of each Vinalogy, or the suggestions below. Once you get used to the effects of hot versus cool climate on a grape, you may want to see what happens to wines from the cooler parts of hot countries.

Tasting ideas:

* **Cabernet Sauvignon:**
  Coonawarra, Australia Vs Bordeaux, France

* **Pinot Noir:**
  Marlborough, New Zealand Vs Chile Vs Burgundy, France

* **Sauvignon Blanc:**
  Marlborough, New Zealand Vs Loire Valley, France

* **Un-oaked Chardonnay:**
  Casablanca Valley, Chile or Napa Valley, California Vs Chablis, Northern France

* **Shiraz/Syrah (**For a cooler region within a 'hot' country)
  Clare Valley, Australia Vs Barossa Valley, Australia

Old Wine Vs Young Wine

Red wine starts off vibrant red in colour and becomes lighter, more transparent and orangey-brown with age. White wine does the opposite and gets darker, turning deep yellow and golden with age. The older a wine gets, the more the flavours will change until they hit a point where the wine just tastes of vinegar! In winespeak, young wines show more 'primary' aromas and flavours like fresh fruit. Wines with a few years of age on them show 'secondary' and 'tertiary' aromas and flavours such as honey, leather, tobacco and caramel.

Tasting ideas:

* Take two bottles of exactly the same wine where the <u>only</u> difference is the year (vintage). Try to get at least four years between them if you can.

* If these are too difficult to find, aim just for the same grape from the same region with a substantial difference in age. The more non-variables there are though, the better.

* Riesling is a fabulous grape to do this experiment with. Watch the white lime blossom turn into rubber, kerosene and lime juice.

Chapter 7

WINE TOP TRUMPS

Wines named after places and styles, not grapes

As mentioned earlier, many wine regions – especially those in Europe – are synonymous with particular grape varieties. Getting to know the famous ones is important because most of the best-known European wines will be labelled after the place they come from, rather than the grapes used to make them.

Here's a list of the wines that I feel you are most likely to see on wine lists, in wine shops and hear about outside of the countries themselves. Only the most widely used grape varieties for each region have been noted. I've added a '+' to indicate where other, often local grape varieties, are used in smaller quantities, and the names in brackets indicate alternative names for the grapes.

NOTE: This list is not exhaustive or it would have taken up a whole book! An excellent, comprehensive list of appellations and their grape varieties can be found in the appendices of the third edition of *The Oxford Companion To Wine* by Jancis Robinson.

This list is available (free) as a PDF on my website: Winebird.co.uk under 'Useful Wine Bits'. I have also added a PDF of this information arranged according to grape variety as that might also come in useful!

Wine named after production area	Within the greater region of:	Country	Most widely used grape(s)
Aloxe-Corton (red)	Burgundy	France	Pinot Noir +
Aloxe-Corton (white)	Burgundy	France	Chardonnay
Amarone	Veneto	Italy	Corvina, Rondinella, Molinara +
Anjou (red)	Loire Valley	France	Cabernet Franc, Cabernet Sauvignon +
Anjou (white)	Loire Valley	France	Chenin Blanc +
Asti	Piedmont	Italy	Moscato Bianco
Auxey-Duresses (red)	Burgundy	France	Pinot Noir +
Auxey-Duresses (white)	Burgundy	France	Chardonnay +
Bandol (red)	Provence	France	Mourvèdre, Grenache, Cinsault
Bandol (white)	Provence	France	Bourboulenc, Clairette, Ugni Blanc
Banyuls	Languedoc-Roussillon	France	Grenache Noir
Barbaresco	Piedmont	Italy	Nebbiolo +
Bardolino	Veneto	Italy	Corvina, Rondinella, Molinara +
Barolo	Piedmont	Italy	Nebbiolo +
Barsac	Bordeaux	France	Sémillon, Sauvignon Blanc
Beaujolais	Beaujolais	France	Gamay
Beaumes de Venise	Rhône Valley	France	Grenache, Syrah +
Bergerac (red)	South West France	France	Cabernet Sauvignon, Cabernet Franc, Merlot
Bergerac (white)	South West France	France	Sémillon, Sauvignon Blanc, Muscadelle +
Bierzo (red)	Castile and León	Spain	Mencia, Garnacha Tinta, Cariñena +
Bierzo (white)	Castile and León	Spain	Godello, Doña Blanca, Malvasia +
Bolgheri (red)	Tuscany	Italy	Cabernet Sauvignon, Merlot, Sangiovese

Bolgheri (white)	Tuscany	Italy	Trebbiano, Vermentino, Sauvignon Blanc
Bonnezeaux	Loire Valley	France	Chenin Blanc
Bordeaux (left bank)	Bordeaux	France	Cabernet Sauvignon, Merlot +
Bordeaux (right bank)	Bordeaux	France	Merlot, Cabernet Sauvignon +
Bordeaux (white)	Bordeaux	France	Sémillon, Sauvignon Blanc +
Bourgueil	Loire Valley	France	Cabernet Franc
Brouilly	Beaujolais	France	Gamay
Brunello (a clone of Sangiovese)	Tuscany	Italy	Sangiovese
Burgundy (red)	Burgundy	France	Pinot Noir
Burgundy (white)	Burgundy	France	Chardonnay
Buzet (red)	South West France	France	Cabernet Sauvignon, Cabernet Franc, Merlot
Buzet (white)	South West France	France	Sauvignon Blanc, Sémillon
Cabardès	Languedoc-Roussillon	France	Grenache, Syrah, Cinsault +
Cahors	South West France	France	Malbec +
Carmignano	Tuscany	Italy	Sangiovese +
Cava	Catalonia	Spain	Macabeo, Parellada, Xarel-lo +
Chablis	Burgundy	France	Chardonnay
Chambolle-Musigny	Burgundy	France	Pinot Noir +
Champagne	Champagne	France	Chardonnay, Pinot Noir, Pinot Meunier
Chassagne-Montrachet	Burgundy	France	Chardonnay
Châteauneuf-du-Pape (red)	Rhône Valley South	France	Grenache, Syrah, Mourvèdre +
Châteauneuf-du-Pape (white)	Rhône Valley South	France	Grenache Blanc, Bourboulenc, Roussanne +
Chénas	Beaujolais	France	Gamay
Cheverney (red)	Loire Valley	France	Gamay, Pinot Noir +
Cheverney (white)	Loire Valley	France	Sauvignon Blanc

Chianti	Tuscany	Italy	Sangiovese +
Chinon (white)	Loire Valley	France	Chenin Blanc
Chinon (red)	Loire Valley	France	Cabernet Franc
Chiroubles	Beaujolais	France	Gamay
Chorey-les-Beaune	Burgundy	France	Pinot Noir +
Cigales	Cigales	Spain	Tempranillo, Garnacha +
Condrieu	Rhône Valley North	France	Viognier
Corbières (red)	Languedoc-Roussillon	France	Carignan, Grenache, Cinsault +
Corbières (white)	Languedoc-Roussillon	France	Bourboulenc, Clairette Blanche, Grenache Blanc +
Cornas	Rhône Valley North	France	Syrah
Costières de Nîmes	Languedoc-Roussillon	France	Carignan, Grenache, Mourvèdre +
Coteaux du Languedoc (red)	Languedoc-Roussillon	France	Carignan, Grenache, Cinsault +
Coteaux du Languedoc (white)	Languedoc-Roussillon	France	Grenache Blanc, Clairette, Bourboulenc +
Côte de Brouilly	Beaujolais	France	Gamay
Côtes de Blaye	Bordeaux	France	Sémillon, Sauvignon Blanc, Muscadelle +
Côtes du Frontonais	South West France	France	Négrette
Coteaux du Layon	Loire Valley	France	Chenin Blanc
Côtes du Luberon (red)	Rhône Valley	France	Grenache, Syrah, Mourvèdre +
Côtes du Luberon (white)	Rhône Valley	France	Grenache Blanc, Clairette, Bourboulenc +
Côtes de Provence (red)	Provence	France	Carignan, Cinsault, Grenache +
Côtes de Provence (white)	Provence	France	Bourboulenc, Clairette, Ugni Blanc
Côtes du Roussillon (red)	Languedoc-Roussillon	France	Carignan, Cinsault, Grenache +

Name	Region	Country	Grapes
Côtes du Roussillon (white)	Languedoc-Roussillon	France	Grenache Blanc, Macabeu Blanc +
Côte-Rôtie	Rhône Valley North	France	Syrah (Viognier)
Côtes du Rhône (red)	Rhône Valley	France	Grenache, Syrah, Mourvèdre +
Côtes du Rhône (white)	Rhône Valley	France	Grenache Blanc, Clairette, Marsanne +
Crozes-Hermitage	Rhône Valley North	France	Syrah
Entre-Deux-Mers	Bordeaux	France	Sémillon, Sauvignon Blanc, Muscadelle +
Faugères (red)	Languedoc-Roussillon	France	Carignan, Cinsault, Grenache +
Faugères (white)	Languedoc-Roussillon	France	Grenache Blanc, Roussanne, Marsanne +
Fitou	Languedoc-Roussillon	France	Carignan, Grenache, Mourvèdre +
Fixin	Burgundy	France	Pinot Noir +
Fleurie	Beaujolais	France	Gamay
Franciacorta	Lombardy	Italy	Chardonnay, Pinot Bianco, Pinot Nero +
Fronsac	Bordeaux	France	Cabernet Sauvignon, Cabernet Franc, Merlot +
Gaillac	South West France	France	Duras, Fer, Servadou +
Gattinara	Piedmont	Italy	Nebbiolo +
Gavi	Piedmont	Italy	Cortese
Gevrey-Chambertin	Burgundy	France	Pinot Noir +
Gigondas	Rhône Valley South	France	Grenache, Syrah, Mourvèdre +
Givry (red)	Burgundy	France	Pinot Noir +
Givry (white)	Burgundy	France	Chardonnay +
Graves (white)	Bordeaux	France	Sémillon, Sauvignon Blanc, Muscadelle
Graves (red)	Bordeaux	France	Cabernet Sauvignon, Cabernet Franc, Merlot +

Hermitage (red)	Rhône Valley North	France	Syrah
Hermitage (white)	Rhône Valley North	France	Marsanne, Roussanne
Juliénas	Beaujolais	France	Gamay
Jumilla (red)	Murcia	Spain	Monastrell +
Jumilla (white)	Murcia	Spain	Airén +
Jurançon	South West France	France	Gros Manseng, Petit Manseng, Courbu +
Ladoix (red)	Burgundy	France	Pinot Noir +
Ladoix (white)	Burgundy	France	Chardonnay +
Liebfraumilch	Rheinhessen, Pfaltz, Nahe & Rheingau	Germany	Riesling, Sylvaner +
Limoux	South West France	France	Petit Manseng, Gros Manseng +
Lirac (red)	Rhône Valley South	France	Grenache, Syrah, Mourvèdre +
Lirac (white)	Rhône Valley South	France	Clairette, Grenache Blanc, Bourboulenc
Loupiac	Bordeaux	France	Sémillon, Sauvignon Blanc, Muscadelle +
Mâcon	Burgundy	France	Chardonnay
Madiran	South West France	France	Tannat +
Marcillac	South West France	France	Fer, Servadou +
Margaux	Bordeaux	France	Cabernet Sauvignon, Cabernet Franc, Merlot +
Marsannay	Burgundy	France	Pinot Noir
Médoc	Bordeaux	France	Cabernet Sauvignon, Merlot +
Menetou-Salon (red)	Loire Valley	France	Pinot Noir
Menetou-Salon (white)	Loire Valley	France	Sauvignon Blanc
Mercurey (red)	Burgundy	France	Pinot Noir +
Mercurey (white)	Burgundy	France	Chardonnay
Meursault	Burgundy	France	Chardonnay
Minervois (red)	Languedoc-Roussillon	France	Grenache, Syrah, Mourvèdre +

Minervois (white)	Languedoc-Roussillon	France	Grenache Blanc, Bourboulenc, Macabeu Blanc +
Monbazillac	South West France	France	Sémillon, Sauvignon Blanc, Muscadelle
Montagny	Burgundy	France	Chardonnay
Montefalco	Lombardy	Italy	Sagrantino
Montepulciano	Abruzzo	Italy	Montepulciano
Monthélie (red)	Burgundy	France	Pinot Noir +
Monthélie (white)	Burgundy	France	Chardonnay +
Morgon	Beaujolais	France	Gamay
Morey St-Denis	Burgundy	France	Pinot Noir +
Moulin-à-Vent	Beaujolais	France	Gamay
Muscadet	Loire Valley	France	Melon de Bourgogne
Navarra (red)	Navarra	Spain	Tempranillo, Garnacha Tinto, Cabernet Sauvignon +
Navarra (white)	Navarra	Spain	Viura +
Nuits-St-Georges	Burgundy	France	Pinot Noir
Orvieto	Umbria	Italy	Trebbiano Toscano, Verdello, Grechetto +
Pauillac	Bordeaux	France	Cabernet Sauvignon, Merlot +
Penedès (red)	Catalonia	Spain	Tempranillo, Garnacha Tinto, Cabernet Franc +
Penedès (white)	Catalonia	Spain	Parellada, Xarel-lo, Macabeo +
Pernand-Vergelesses (red)	Burgundy	France	Pinot Noir +
Pernand-Vergelesses (white)	Burgundy	France	Chardonnay +
Pessac-Léognan	Bordeaux	France	Sémillon, Sauvignon Blanc, Muscadelle
Pomerol	Bordeaux	France	Merlot, Cabernet Sauvignon +
Pomino	Tuscany	Italy	Sangiovese +
Pommard	Burgundy	France	Pinot Noir +
Port	Douro Valley	Portugal	Touriga Nacional, Touriga Franca, Bastardo +

Pouilly-Fuissé	Burgundy	France	Chardonnay
Pouilly-Fumé	Loire Valley	France	Sauvignon Blanc
Priorat (red)	Catalonia	Spain	Garnacha Tinta +
Priorat (white)	Catalonia	Spain	Garnacha Blanca +
Prosecco	Veneto	Italy	Glera
Puligny-Montrachet	Burgundy	France	Chardonnay
Quarts de Chaume	Loire Valley	France	Chenin Blanc
Quincy	Loire Valley	France	Sauvignon Blanc
Régnié	Beaujolais	France	Gamay
Reuilly	Loire Valley	France	Sauvignon Blanc
Rias Baixas	Galicia	Spain	Albariño
Ribera del Duero	Ribera del Duero	Spain	Tempranillo (Tinto Fino) +
Rioja	Rioja	Spain	Tempranillo, Garnacha +
Rueda	Rueda	Spain	Verdejo, Virua, Sauvignon Blanc +
Roero (red)	Piedmont	Italy	Nebbiolo
Roero (white)	Piedmont	Italy	Arneis
Rully (red)	Burgundy	France	Pinot Noir +
Rully (white)	Burgundy	France	Chardonnay
Saint-Chinian	Languedoc-Roussillon	France	Grenache, Syrah, Mourvèdre +
Salice Salentino (red)	Puglia	Italy	Negroamaro +
Salice Salentino (white)	Puglia	Italy	Chardonnay
Sancerre (red)	Loire Valley	France	Pinot Noir
Sancerre (white)	Loire Valley	France	Sauvignon Blanc
Santenay (red)	Burgundy	France	Pinot Noir +
Santenay (white)	Burgundy	France	Chardonnay +
Sassicaia	Tuscany	Italy	Cabernet Sauvignon
Sauternes	Bordeaux	France	Sauvignon Blanc, Sémillon
Saumur (Red)	Loire Valley	France	Cabernet Franc, Cabernet Sauvignon +
Saumur-Champigny (Red)	Loire Valley	France	Cabernet Franc, Cabernet Sauvignon +
Savennières	Loire Valley	France	Chenin Blanc
Savigny-lès-Beaune (red)	Burgundy	France	Pinot Noir +

Name	Region	Country	Grapes
Savigny-lès-Beaune (white)	Burgundy	France	Chardonnay +
Sherry	Sherry (Jerez)	Spain	Palomino Fino
Soave	Veneto	Italy	Garganega, Pinot Bianco +
St-Aubin (red)	Burgundy	France	Pinot Noir +
St-Aubin (white)	Burgundy	France	Chardonnay +
St-Émilion	Bordeaux	France	Merlot, Cabernet Sauvignon +
St-Estèphe	Bordeaux	France	Cabernet Sauvignon, Merlot +
St-Bris	Chablis	France	Sauvignon Blanc, Sauvignon Gris
St-Joseph (red)	Rhône Valley	France	Syrah
St-Joseph (white)	Rhône Valley	France	Marsanne, Roussanne
St-Julien	Bordeaux	France	Cabernet Sauvignon, Merlot +
St-Nicolas-de-Bourgueil	Loire Valley	France	Cabernet Franc
St-Romain (red)	Burgundy	France	Pinot Noir +
St-Romain (white)	Burgundy	France	Chardonnay +
St-Véran	Burgundy	France	Chardonnay
Tavel	Rhône Valley	France	Grenache, Cinsault +
Tokaji	Tokaj	Hungary	Furmint, Harslevelu
Touraine (red)	Loire Valley	France	Cabernet Franc, Cabernet Sauvignon +
Touraine	Loire Valley	France	Chenin Blanc, Sauvignon Blanc +
Vacqueyras (red)	Rhône Valley	France	Grenache, Syrah, Mourvèdre +
Vacqueyras (white)	Rhône Valley	France	Grenache Blanc, Clairette, Bourboulenc +
Valdepeñas	Castilla-La-Mancha	Spain	Tempranillo (Cencibel)
Valpolicella	Veneto	Italy	Corvina, Rondinella, Molinara +
Valtellina Superiore	Lombardy	Italy	Nebbiolo

Vino Nobile di Montepulciano	Tuscany	Italy	Sangiovese +
Vinsobres	Rhône Valley South	France	Grenache, Syrah, Mourvèdre +
Volnay	Burgundy	France	Pinot Noir +
Vosne-Romanée	Burgundy	France	Pinot Noir +
Vougeot (red)	Burgundy	France	Pinot Noir +
Vougeot (white)	Burgundy	France	Chardonnay +
Vouvray	Loire Valley	France	Chenin Blanc

About the author

Helena Nicklin was bitten by the wine bug while studying in Rome as part of her language degree. On returning to London, she joined the crew at the infamous Vingt Fine Wine Fanatics in London selling some of the finest wines on the planet. Then, after several years of intense tasting 'practice', she joined the glorious people at Decanter Magazine and more recently, wine merchant Corney & Barrow, where she negotiated prices, tasted samples and wrote wine copy as part of the commercial buying team. During this time, she also completed the WSET Diploma in wines & spirits. Yes, she got paid to do what is essentially a degree in booze.

In October 2011, she combined all her passions (wine, writing and performing) to set up her own company: Winebird. Now, she runs VINALOGY-style wine tastings around London, is a freelance writer and has her own YouTube wine channel to educate beginners in her own, original way. Helena lives in East Dulwich with her 'winehusband' Hamish, Ludwig the winespaniel, winebaby Ivy and winebump tbc!

Winebird.co.uk
Winebird.org
Twitter: @TheWinebird
G+: +Helena Nicklin

About the illustrator

Olivia Whitworth is an illustrator who recently graduated with a Masters in Illustration from Camberwell College of Art. Since then she has thrown herself in to the freelance life and undertaken a diverse range of jobs, both in size and styles. Having originally trained in Architecture, Olivia's illustrations often like to incorporate bits of the built environment but in a less rigid and technical way than an architectural drawing. Her usual weapon of choice when working is a simple black ink ballpoint, often combined with watercolours which allow a little more looseness behind more carefully drawn black lines. Olivia was born and bred in Sheffield, but is currently living in London with her boyfriend where they are trying to find a hypoallergenic cat to keep Livi company during the day.

Liviwhit.com
Twitter: @livi_whitworth
Instagram @liviwhit